NEW DIMENSIONS IN
BEAD AND WIRE JEWELRY
UNEXPECTED COMBINATIONS • UNIQUE DESIGNS

MARGOT POTTER

NORTH LIGHT BOOKS

North Light Books
CINCINNATI, OHIO

www.fwmedia.com

15   14   13   12   11   5   4   3   2   1

DISTRIBUTED IN CANADA BY FRASER DIRECT
100 Armstrong Avenue
Georgetown, ON, Canada L7G 5S4
Tel: (905) 877-4411

DISTRIBUTED IN THE U.K. AND EUROPE BY F&W MEDIA
INTERNATIONAL
Brunel House, Newton Abbot, Devon, TQ12 4PU, England
Tel: (+44) 1626 323200, Fax: (+44) 1626 323319
Email: enquiries@fwmedia.com

DISTRIBUTED IN AUSTRALIA BY CAPRICORN LINK
P.O. Box 704, S. Windsor NSW, 2756 Australia
Tel: (02) 4577-3555

ISBN-13: 978-1-4403-0924-3
ISBN-10: 1-4403-0924-8

Editor: Rachel Scheller
Designer: Kelly O'Dell
Production Coordinator: Greg Nock
Photographers: Christine Polomsky, Ric Deliantoni
Photo Stylist: Lauren Emmerling

METRIC CONVERSION CHART

To convert	to	multiply by
Inches	Centimeters	2.54
Centimeters	Inches	0.4
Feet	Centimeters	30.5
Centimeters	Feet	0.03
Yards	Meters	0.9
Meters	Yards	1.1

ABOUT THE AUTHOR

Margot Potter has written six popular and humorous how-to-design titles for North Light Books. She's an author, designer, freelance writer, video host, consultant, TV spokesperson and jewelry-making expert with over 20 years of experience. She designs, blogs, creates video and consults for a wide variety of manufacturers and companies in the DIY craft industry. Her impatient, impetuous approach to design resonates with people who long for creative expression but lack the time and focus to spend hours on a single creation. Margot is a pied piper of creativity who encourages people to color outside of the lines and live out loud. You can find out more about Margot and view her internationally popular blog and samples of her work at www.margotpotter.com.

THIS IS DEDICATED TO THE ONE I LOVE

I dedicate this book to my endlessly patient and beloved husband, Drew. You have supported me, held my hand, lifted me up, cheered me on, made me laugh, dried my tears, picked up my slack, poured me a drink, swept, mopped, packed, shipped, cleaned, and cared for and fed our menagerie and our daughter. But most of all, you've loved me even when I'm at my worst and inspired me to strive every moment of every day to become my best.

ACKNOWLEDGMENTS

No book gets made without a team of people to help make it happen. I am so grateful to the folks from Beadalon for their ongoing support. (Special thanks to Mike Shields, Mike Hogan, John Fritzinger, Wyatt White, Yvette Rodriguez and Vlad Alvarez.) IMHO, there is no finer or more forthright wire manufacturer in the world. Period. They make a stellar product and they do it in factories right here in the good old US of A.

Thank you to the entire team at F+W Media/North Light Books, including my delightful new editor, Rachel Scheller; my acquisitions editor, the wonderful Tonia Davenport; and the wickedly witty editorial director, Christine Doyle. Thanks to Greg Hatfield and Sarah Reynolds for your PR wizardry, and to Tom Todd for getting my books into as many hands as possible. Hugs and kisses to my favorite photographer, Christine Polomsky. Thanks to the book designer, Kelly O'Dell, and the entire team of photographers and editors who made this book shine. To my friend Fernando DaSilva, who brought me a huge box of gorgeous beads at the exact moment I needed them—thank you. And finally and most of all, I want to thank my lovely, talented, wonderful daughter Avalon for *yet again* giving up a good portion of her "Mommy and Me" time this summer so I could write another book. It is not possible that anyone in the universe loves their child as much as I love mine. Thank you for making the most fabulous design in this book. You amaze me.

TABLE OF CONTENTS

INTRODUCTION

I have always been a dimensional thinker. My jewelry designs reflect this. I like to think of my designs as sculptures and the wire and beads as my armatures and clay. I've been working with shaping and beading wire for over ten years now, and I never cease to find new ways to use them. Wire intrigues me endlessly, not just as a structural element but also as a decorative element. It occurred to me that although there are some excellent books on wire jewelry, no one has explored a sculptural approach or focused on both shaping and beading wire designs and combining the two. So this idea was born. If you like to defy the laws of physics, if you like to take your materials to the edge and if you'd like to find new ways to integrate dimensional elements into your work, then you've found your book.

We'll explore wire wrapping, twisting, coiling, crochet, jigs, chain maille and more. We'll create architecturally and sculpturally inspired designs with beading wire and beads. We'll find new pathways of creative exploration and wander down them to see what we might discover. We'll make some interesting discoveries and a few glorious mistakes. Along the way, we'll hopefully learn some new techniques and form some fresh ideas.

My professional design career began with a wire and bead ornament I created one year for Christmas when we were low on money for gifts. That little ornament led to a sculptural wire design for a catalog cover, and that design led me to query my first book. Here I am, six years later, and it seems apropos to come full circle. I'm excited to have you join me on this new adventure.

**CHEERS,
MARGOT**

EVERYTHING YOU WANTED TO KNOW ABOUT WIRE BUT WERE AFRAID TO ASK

This book focuses on working with two types of wire used in jewelry making. Shaping wire is made from metal that is drawn or pulled through a metal drawing plate into a continuous wire. This wire is used for wrapping, shaping and forming a variety of jewelry items and findings. Beading wire is a multi-stranded, cabled metal wire coated with nylon. It is used for stringing and weaving jewelry.

SHAPING WIRE

Shaping wire is measured in gauges. The gauge refers to the thickness of the wire. The gauge number gets smaller as the wire gets thicker. The thicker the wire, the stiffer and more difficult it is to manipulate; conversely, thicker gauges are stronger and more likely to maintain their shape. You will use a variety of gauges while working with the techniques in this book.

Copper-coated wire: The majority of the wire featured in this book is Artistic Wire, which is a copper wire with a colorful or plated coating. Some is silver-plated, some is coated with vivid metallic colors, and some is gold-plated. Artistic Wire is the perfect choice for beginners because of its affordability and versatility. Most coated copper wire has a thin nylon coating to prevent chipping, scratching and tarnishing.

Copper is soft, easy to manipulate and can be work-hardened into a sturdy and stable shape. Work hardening refers to the process of strengthening the metal's structure as you bend, hammer and shape it, due to the friction these actions cause. All wire can be over-hardened, at which point it becomes brittle; practicing with the wire will help prevent this from happening.

Base metal wire: Some of the projects in the book feature natural copper, brass and stainless steel wire. Unlike Artistic Wire, these wires are not metal-plated or color-coated, but they are usually nylon-coated to prevent tarnish. Copper is the most malleable and,

as I mentioned, is a great choice for beginners. Brass wire is also very malleable and is another affordable and easy-to-use option, especially if you want the look of aged gold in your pieces. Stainless steel wire is less malleable but maintains a great deal of strength and is far less susceptible to the tarnish you will get from copper or brass. I like base metal wire for wrapping, and I find stainless steel to be a little too stiff for my preference, although other people I know swear by it. Check out the new square and half-round copper-coated wires; they are life-changing for wire-wrapped designs!

Annealed iron wire: This wire is rather stiff, rusty and rustic. Still, I do love it, and it's sturdy stuff indeed. It's found at hardware stores in big rolls. Wipe the rust off with a polishing cloth so your jewelry doesn't make the wearer rusty.

Sterling silver and gold wire: Sterling silver and gold wire are made from precious metals. Precious metal wire comes in three different levels of stiffness: hard, half-hard and dead soft. The stiffness of this wire is measured on a scale from 0–4, working from softest to hardest. The wire becomes stiffer the more it is drawn through the draw plate. Dead soft wire is great for free-form wirework, wrapping around a base, and knitting, weaving and crocheting. It doesn't retain its shape as well as harder wires. Half-hard wire works well for sharp-edged corners, findings and wrapped bases and more permanent forms, and many people prefer this for wire wrapping. Hard wire is stiffer and has a spring to it, so it maintains a shape with the greatest level of permanence, though it is the most difficult to manipulate. Most designers work with dead soft or half-hard, and it becomes a personal preference in terms of how they use these wires. If you've mastered using the base metal wires and you want to take your work upscale, you'll want to explore sterling and gold wire. It's expensive but beautiful. It's best to know what you're doing so you don't end up with a pile of twisted wreckage. Practice with base metal, and then graduate to precious metal. Or, if you're like me, work with whatever strikes your fancy and fits your bank account. If you want a more upscale, fine product, precious metal wire will deliver.

Titanium wire: This is the most flexible, malleable wire with which I've ever worked. It's great for satisfying wire projects, and it comes in a variety of vibrant colors. It won't provide the same strength or structure as other wires, but it's a fun material to add to your coffers.

Memory wire: Memory wire is a stainless steel wire that has been permanently formed into a shape. It's a perfect foundation wire that retains its stiffness, and it can also be cut into small segments that can be beaded and added to designs.

BEADING WIRE

Beading wire is measured in diameter and strand count. The diameter refers to the thickness of the wire, and as the numbers get bigger, the wire gets thicker. The strand count refers to the number of cabled wires inside each nylon-coated tube. Beading wire is created on machines that cable, coat and spool. The higher the strand count of your wire, the more supple and flexible the wire will be.

Stainless steel cabled wire: The majority of beading wire on the market is fashioned from tiny, cabled, stainless steel wires coated in nylon. The wire featured in this book is mostly stainless steel cabled wire. This wire is strong, flexible and can take a fair amount of abuse. Though it is made of steel, you still need to learn a few things to prevent friction or poor finishing techniques from abrading the wire and

causing it to break. Make sure you learn how to crimp properly (see page 17). The most important thing to remember is that the wire needs to fill the hole of your largest bead. If you don't fill that hole, the wire moves around inside while you wear the piece, and that friction causes the nylon coating to wear off. Once that happens, the small cabled wires break down until the entire piece eventually breaks.

Seven-strand wire is used primarily for crafting; it's stiff and it's not as strong as wires with a larger strand count. It can, however, provide structure. It's a good material to practice with because it's very affordable. Nineteen-strand wire gives you a more professional drape and finish and is an economical choice that doesn't compromise on quality. The finest flexibility and drape comes from 49-strand wire.

Colored stainless steel wire: This is the same basic wire as the stainless steel cabled wire, but with a colorful plated coating applied before the nylon, resulting in a virtual rainbow of wire colors. If you do any exposed beading wirework, you'll want an array of these colorful wires.

Sterling silver wire: Sterling wire is made entirely of tiny braided strands of .925 silver. It's gorgeous and very flexible, but it can kink if you overwork it. Use this for beautiful exposed wire designs, but not for weaving.

Plated wire: A 24-carat gold or sterling silver plating is applied to cabled stainless steel wire to create this wire. This is wonderful when left exposed in your designs and is an affordable alternative to sterling wire if you're on a budget.

Crinkle wire: Crinkle wire has a consistent waved pattern permanently created in the wire. You can expose this wire or bead on it. It lends terrific movement to your pieces.

Satin finish copper, silver and gold wire: These are plated wires with a satin metallic finish. They are also ideal for exposed wire designs, and the colors and satin finish work really nicely with base metal shaping wires. You can also get two-tone wires like SilveRose, SilverGold or Champagne for similar purposes.

A BRIEF GUIDE TO FINDING THE RIGHT FINDINGS AND THE BEST BEADS

FINDING OUT ABOUT FINDINGS

Clasps: So many clasps, so little time! Lobster claw, spring ring, hook and eye, S-hook, EZ-Crimp clasps, toggle clasps and so many more! These are the connectors that keep your jewelry together. We'll use finished clasps, and we'll also make some of our own.

Ear wires: These are the curved wires attached to an earring that go through your pierced hole. They come in a huge variety of shapes and sizes, including French wires, dapped wires, coiled wires, hoops, kidney wires, lever backs and earring hinges. We'll use both finished and handmade ear wires.

Jump rings: Jump rings connect things together. They are metal rings with a split that opens and closes to attach different components. It is important to open and close jump rings properly and create tension so they remain closed (see page 14). We'll also learn how to make our own (see page 15).

Chain: Chain has become *de rigueur* for jewelry designers over the past several years. It adds texture, interest and movement to your work. We will use premade chains and forge a few of our own.

Crimp beads and tubes: These little metal beads or tubes are used to connect beading wire to a clasp. They can also station beads on a wire or be used as spacers between larger beads. There are special tools designed specifically for crimping, and they'll help create strong and long-lasting finishes.

Loop crimp ends: Loop crimps are a combination of a crimp tube with a soldered loop on the end that is easy to connect to a clasp with a jump ring. These are great for lighter weight beaded designs.

Scrimps: Scrimps are metal tubes with a threaded screw that is tightened to secure the wire. There are Scrimps with loops to connect them and Scrimps that finish memory wire. They take just a little practice, but it's well worth the effort.

EZ-Crimps: An EZ-Crimp end is a tube with a loop on it, reinforced with thicker metal sides. EZ-Crimps can come with clasps attached or without. They are easy to secure using an EZ-Crimp tool or a Mighty Crimp Tool. I use these constantly, especially when I want a clean finish on a bracelet.

Wire Guardians: These curved tubes secure your beading wire and protect it from abrasion at the clasp. They're particularly fabulous for bracelets and beaded watchbands.

Crimp covers: Crimp covers are split hollow metal beads used to conceal crimp beads and tubes. Use a Mighty Crimp Tool to compress them closed around the crimps. They give a nice clean finish to your work and hide crimps in stationed wire designs.

BEADS TO DECORATE YOUR WIRES

When working with shaping wire, it's important to remember that the tension you are creating can stress and break your beads. If you want to use more delicate beads like blown glass or crystal, I suggest you practice with plastic and work your way up to them. There is nothing more disappointing than breaking an expensive bead, especially if it is a one-of-a-kind creation. Or, even worse—and this has happened to me—getting a tiny piece of glass stuck in your eye.

Glass and crystal: Glass beads can be cast, blown, molded, pressed, lampworked or torched. They come in a seemingly endless variety of colors, sizes, shapes and finishes. Some are artist-crafted and are exquisite and precious, so care should be taken when working with them. Some come from factories in the Czech Republic and are both affordable and lovely. There are less expensive glass beads coming from China, but remember that you get what you pay for. I'm a believer in using the best-quality materials I can afford.

I use SWAROVSKI ELEMENTS for the crystal in my designs. I've worked with this product for a number of years, and there is nothing that compares. The color, cut, light play and beauty of leaded crystal is superior. Take care, though, when working with this material, because if you put too much tension on it, it will chip or break. The sparkle of crystal against a hammered or exposed wire design is a very pleasing combination.

Plastic: To say I'm a fan of plastic is a vast understatement—I love it! I cannot get enough of big, bodacious, retrofabulous plastic beads. I love them because they're sturdy and strong, big and bold, and so lightweight that you can use them to excess in your work. There are a variety of vintage plastics, of which the most prevalent and currently popular is Lucite. Others are created from acrylic, resin, catalan, Plexiglas, Bakelite and celluloid. The nice thing about working with plastic is that it's a bit more forgiving to the novice designer. It's less likely to chip or crack than glass or crystal, and it can look equally as lovely if you buy good-quality beads.

Semi-precious stones: When I work with gemstone beads, I work with semi-precious stones. There are so many simply gorgeous mineral and stone beads for the choosing and most of them are surprisingly affordable. You can get them in all sorts of colors, shapes and sizes. They can be carved, pierced or inlaid.

Art beads: It's hard to summarize art beads into a few sentences. There are entire books devoted to the many kinds of art beads, and there are huge shows you can attend to meet the artisans and hand-select their wares. These beads come in many materials including glass, porcelain, ceramic, precious metal clay, precious metal, polymer clay, pewter . . . and the list goes on. Supporting the art bead community means supporting an artist who is working tirelessly to create original, unique, exquisite beads for your designs. That's something to embrace!

Ceramic: Ceramic, porcelain and clay beads have been made for hundreds of years. Depending on how they are made and finished, they are, for the most part, very sturdy. I particularly enjoy ceramic focal beads because they give my work so much dimension and color.

Cubic zirconia: Cubic zirconia (or CZ) beads have been popular over the last few years as an alternative to cut crystal. They have a lot of fire and sparkle and can be affordable. They are also stronger than crystal or glass.

Wood and organic elements: Wood, shell, nut, bone and other organic beads are plentiful, affordable and lightweight. I'm particularly fond of the organic beads from the Philippines. I'm also a fan of the delicately carved Ojime beads from Japan. There are many gorgeous carved bone beads from China. These all work well with wire for a more organic and earthy design aesthetic.

Focal elements: A focal element refers to a bead or pendant that is the focal point of your design. They can be a fantastic source of design inspiration and can make ho-hum design sing. You'll find a lot of focal beads on the market, and I suggest you collect them. They'll greatly inform the rest of your beads in terms of color, scale, texture, shape and material.

TOOLS FOR GETTING WIRED

Working with wire requires a small arsenal of tools. As you progress, your tool selection expands. It is always my suggestion that you start with less expensive tools until you master your medium, and then progress to higher quality tools as your pocket book allows. For me, there are never, ever enough tools. It becomes an obsession.

Chasing or ball-peen hammer: This is a hammer with a flat side for hammering wire flat and a ball or peen side for creating texture. Good chasing hammers don't leave marks on your wire when you use them; less well-designed hammers have sharper edges. I often like to follow the flattening with the texturing. You can also find textured hammers that will create a variety of textured finishes in wire or sheet metal.

Miniature anvil: You'll find a small-scale anvil useful as a surface for hammering smaller objects and for forming rounder shapes. I have several in my studio.

Steel bench block: This small steel block is square and flat on all sides. It is used as a surface for hammering. You can do without a miniature anvil for most of the projects in this book, but you really need a steel bench block. Once you start hammering things, you'll be happy you have one. It's addictive.

Bench block pad: This sand-filled, leather pad helps to deaden the relentless noise of hammering. You need one. Your eardrums, your family and your pets will thank you.

Wire jigs: Wire jigs have a series of holes and various sizes of pegs you can insert to create stationed dowels for making shapes with wire. There are many, many kinds of jigs, even ones that form words from wire.

Jump ring maker tool: Jump rings are wonderful things, and sometimes you wish you had one in the same color, gauge or finish as the wire you used in a project. The jump ring maker tool allows you to create your own jump rings. You can purchase dowels in a variety of diameters and shapes. I love using this tool to make wire coils, too.

Dowels: Necessity is the mother of invention, and in my studio, absolutely anything can be used as a dowel for my wire work. Pill containers, wire and thread spools, rat tail combs . . . even a powder brush jumped in to save the day for me recently. There are, of course, dowels you can purchase that are specifically made for jewelry making. You will find that no matter how many you own, at some point you'll be improvising to get the shape you desire.

Wire rounder: The wire rounder has a burr cup end that rounds sharp wire ends. This is particularly useful for ear wires and jewelry hooks. Sharp wire ends are scratchy!

Ring mandrel: A ring mandrel can be made from a variety of materials. A metal mandrel will work best for wire wrapping rings. I tend to use the size larger than I need while making my initial wraps, as the ring will be a size smaller once you finish wrapping. Working on the mandrel, especially with softer wire, helps maintain the shape and size of a ring.

Knitting spool: There are all sorts of knitting spools, from rustic wooden handles with nails hammered into them to the more sophisticated spool I feature in the book. They all work in pretty much the same way; it's a matter of preference. They are used for weaving wire into a tube. You can use shaping wire or beading wire, but use a thin gauge for the best results.

Crochet hooks: I'm sure you know what a crochet hook is, but did you know that it's easy and fun to crochet shaping wire? Well, it is! Again, thin wire gauges of shaping or beading work best here.

Memory wire shears: These shears are designed specifically to cut memory wire. They're also handy for stainless steel and annealed iron wire. You can use them while making jump rings with thicker wire to get a flush cut on both sides.

Flush cutters: Flush cutters have a beveled interior jaw and a flat or flush exterior. These are used to cut wires. They leave a small beveled end on one side, so be sure to go back and cut the beveled side flush when working with shaping wire.

Round-nose pliers: Round-nose pliers have a round- or conical-shaped jaw. They are used for creating loops and turning wires.

Chain-nose pliers: Chain-nose pliers have a flat jaw with a pointed end. They are used for grasping, pulling and tucking wire.

Bent-nose pliers: Bent-nose pliers have a longer, thinner jaw than chain-nose pliers do, and, as the name implies, the jaw is bent. These are favored by many chain maille workers when combined with a pair of chain-nose pliers to assist in opening and closing jump rings.

Flat-nose pliers: Flat-nose pliers have a thick, wide jaw. These are great for grasping, securing and pulling thick shaping wires.

Nylon jaw pliers: Nylon jaw pliers have a thick, wide jaw made of nylon. This allows you to straighten long pieces of wire without nicking or chipping the finish.

Crimp tool (Mighty, regular and micro): Crimp tools are designed for use with crimp beads and tubes. They come in three sizes that coordinate with the various crimp sizes. You can also use the Mighty Crimp Tool for closing crimp covers and securing EZ-Crimps.

EZ-Crimp tool: The EZ-Crimp tool is designed specifically for use with an EZ-Crimp end. The round shape inside the jaws is used to compress the EZ-Crimp closed.

Scrimp tool: The Scrimp tool is a tiny screwdriver used to secure the tiny screws on Scrimp findings.

Bead boards: A bead board is the perfect place to design your jewelry, hold your beads and findings, and keep everything organized. Everyone who makes beaded jewelry needs a bead board; actually, several!

Tacky mat: This super-sticky, double-sided mat is the perfect place to secure small wire pieces or beads and prevent them from running away. (They'll do that when you're not looking.) It can be washed and used over and over again.

Polishing cloth: A polishing cloth removes tarnish as you straighten your wire. It also protects your fingers from the wire as you straighten it.

Jewelry cleaning solution: When working with copper, brass, sterling or gold-plated wire, there will be tarnish. To remove tarnish after you complete your work, use a good jewelry cleaning solution. Spray, set, rinse and remove any residue with a soft cloth.

Two-hole punch: A two-hole punch makes super quick work of drilling holes into thick metal components. It has a small and large punch. I can't believe I ever lived without this tool.

Protective eyewear: You're working with wire and beads. Sometime, someday, something will shoot itself at your eyes. Eyes are important. Wear goggles or other protective eyewear as you work.

Visors or CraftOptics lenses: Working on intricate projects in a small scale can place tremendous strain on your eyes. By wearing a visor with magnification, or by having special optical-quality lenses set in glasses tailored to your eyeglass prescription, you'll reduce eye strain and be able to focus on those small details.

TECHNIQUES

When it comes to working with wire, technique is everything. Shoddy workmanship, or what they call "user error," is almost always behind problems in finished pieces. It's tantamount to your success and your sanity that you practice, practice and practice some more until you have mastered the basic techniques. Did I mention that you need to practice?

OPENING AND CLOSING JUMP RINGS

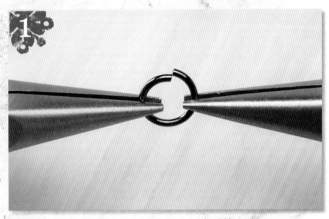

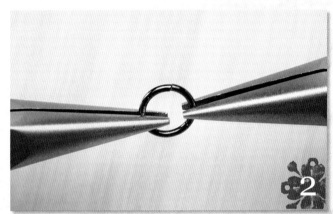

Begin by grasping the jump ring on both sides with two pairs of chain-nose pliers, or with chain-nose pliers and bent-nose pliers. Open the jump ring laterally, moving one end toward you and one end away from you. Don't open widthwise, as this changes the shape of the ring.

To close the ring, grasp it again on both sides with the pliers. Gently compress the ends together as you bring them past one another. Continue gently compressing them as you bring them back together. When they come together the second time, you should hear and feel a click. This indicates that the ring is closed with tension and will remain closed until you open it again. If it doesn't click, brush the ends past one another again until you secure them with tension.

SHAPING AND HAMMERING WIRE

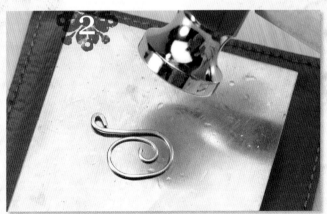

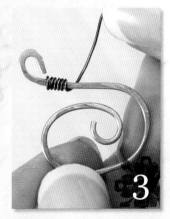

Use round-nose pliers or your fingers to create coils and loops in the wire.

Place the shape on a steel bench block with a bench block pad beneath it. Use the flat end of the chasing hammer to flatten the shape. Use the round or peen end if you want to create texture.

To wrap smaller gauge wire around the shape, make your first wrap, cut off excess wire and coil tightly around the core wire. Use chain-nose pliers to tuck in the wire tails. This is all about tension, and the more you create, the more consistent the wraps will look.

CREATING JUMP RINGS

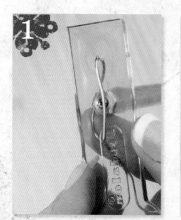

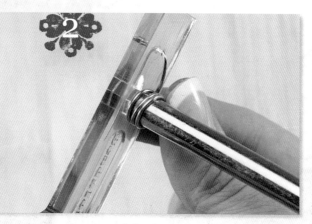

Insert one end of the working wire into the hole on the jump ring maker tool and bend it flush to the back of the tool base. You can work from the spool, or, if you prefer, cut off a length of wire with which you are comfortable working.

Begin wrapping the wire tightly around the dowel, moving up as you work.

Insert your index finger into the finger hole in the tool, secure the wire on the dowel and spin your finger. This allows you to coil the wire around the dowel quickly.

Cut the coil from the tool. Slide the coil off.

Use flush cutters to cut the rings.

Use the flush side of the cutters to flush cut the pointed side of each ring.

CREATING A HOOK AND EYE CLASP

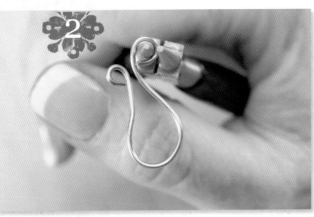

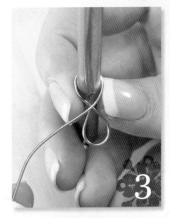

Create a small loop in one end of your wire. Bend it around a round dowel in the desired size.

Use round-nose pliers to make a larger loop in the opposite end of the hook. Hammer the wire flat on a steel bench block.

Use another length of wire and a dowel to create an S shape. Bend the wire around the dowel beginning at the center, and repeat on the opposite side.

CREATING AN EAR WIRE

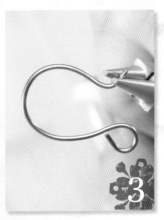

Wrap one end of a 20-gauge wire around a dowel. Here, I've used a larger round dowel for a more rounded ear wire. You can opt to use a small dowel for a more traditional ear wire shape.

Use chain-nose pliers to create a large loop in one end of the shaped wire.

Use round-nose pliers to gently bend the opposite end up as shown.

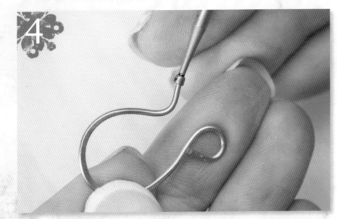

Use a wire rounder tool to gently round the ear wire and prevent it from scratching the ear when worn.

USING A CRIMP TOOL

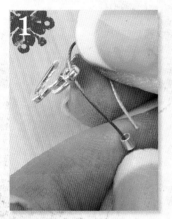

Be sure the tool and the crimp tube are compatible in size. Thread the wire through the tube, through the clasp end and back into the tube. Leave a ⅛" (3mm) loop; if you crimp the wire too closely to the clasp, the wire will wear and break.

Use the front opening in the crimp tool to compress the tube into an oval shape. This keeps the wires uncrossed for crimping. If they are crossed, they can't be crimped into two separate channels.

Use the heart-shaped back opening in the tool to compress the tube, creating two separate wire channels.

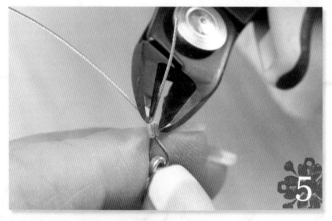

Return to the front opening in the tool, keeping the indented side of the crimp facing outward. Compress to gently fold the two channels together.

Cut off the excess wire flush to the bottom of the tube. I prefer this method to stringing the wire back into the beads. If you can string the wire back into the beads, you're probably not using the right diameter of wire. You should always strive to fill the holes of the beads with the wire to prevent wear.

USING AN EZ-CRIMP

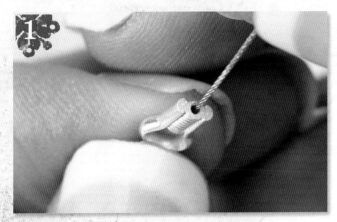

Thread the wire into the opening in the EZ-Crimp.

Use a Mighty Crimp Tool or an EZ-Crimp tool to compress the smooth sides of the channel together. This takes effort; check the wire to be sure it is completely secured, and if not, compress again. Use flush cutters to cut off the excess wire.

USING A SCRIMP

The Scrimp finding has a tiny screw. Use a Scrimp tool to loosen the screw enough to thread the wire into the hole in the Scrimp. If you over-loosen and lose the screw, the tool comes with extras in the shaft. I like to secure the Scrimp with chain-nose pliers if it has a loop at the end, or with the front end of a crimp tool if it does not have a loop end.

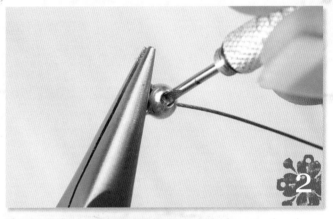

Use the Scrimp tool to tighten the screw and secure the wire. Test the wire to be sure it is secured properly, and if not, continue to tighten until it is.

STATIONING BEADS WITH A CRIMP TUBE

You can use a crimp bead or tube to station beads or sections of beads along a wire. I use a pair of chain-nose pliers in this case, since there won't be two wires in the chambers created by a crimp tool. Crimp tubes on either side of a bead allow you to separate beads along your design.

USING A WIRE JIG

The pegs on the jig are movable, and various configurations result in various shapes. In this case, I'm creating a square. Place the pegs as desired.

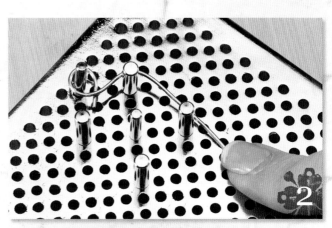

Wrap the wire around the top peg and work around the outside edges of the pegs.

Once you have made your desired shape, secure the other end of the wire by wrapping it around one of the pegs.

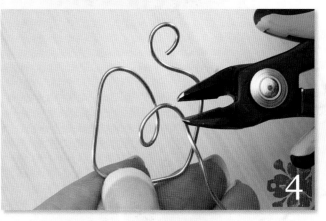

Cut off the wire tail and tuck the tail in with pliers.

CREATING A COILED DANGLE

Insert the shaft of a head pin into a bead and slide it down to the head. Hold the wire flush to the top of the bead with round-nose pliers.

Bend the wire at a 90-degree angle.

Move the pliers onto the bend by turning them upward.

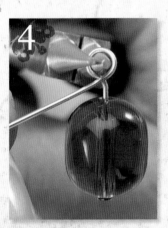

Wrap the wire around the jaw of the round-nose pliers, making a loop.

Grasp the wire with a pair of chain-nose pliers and wrap it tightly, working from the bottom of the loop to the top of the bead.

Cut off the wire tail with flush cutters.

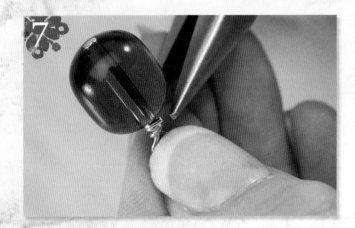

Tuck the tail into the coil with chain-nose pliers.

CREATING A LOOP-TOP DANGLE

Insert the shaft of a head pin into a bead and slide it down to the head. Bend the wire flush to the top of the bead at a 90-degree angle.

Cut off the excess wire to about ¼" (6mm) in length.

Grasp the wire end with round-nose pliers and loop the wire back over itself. Use chain-nose pliers to secure the loop.

MAKING BEADING WIRE CIRCLES

Method 1:

Method 2:

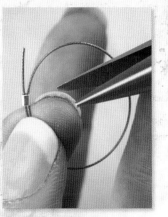

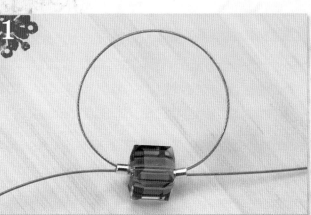

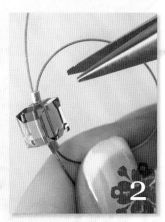

Slide a crimp tube on a wire. Loop the wire to form a circle and thread it back into the opposite end of the tube. Use chain-nose pliers to compress the tube. Cut off the excess wire. You can optionally add beads to the wire circle before crimping.

Thread a crimp tube, a bead and a second crimp tube onto a wire. Loop the wire to form a circle and thread it back through the opposite side of the crimp tube, the bead and the second crimp tube.

Use chain-nose pliers to secure the crimp tubes flush to each side of the bead. Cut the wire ends flush to the crimps.

The key to every successful creation is a strong foundation, in a literal and a figurative sense. If you don't build the right foundation, you will find an endless amount of frustration when things just won't maintain their shape. Shaping wire can be bent, hammered, woven and coiled into a litany of shapes and sculptures. Different widths or gauges of wires in different materials all behave slightly differently. That's part of the fun! We're going to start with the basics and explore some quick and satisfying projects to whet your wire whistle.

With *Gerbera* (see page 24), we'll play with 20-gauge silver-plated wire and beads to make free-form flower shapes. This helps you get a feel for the way wire moves, bends and forms into shapes. 20-gauge copper-coated wire is a great starting point because it's very flexible, but not so malleable that it won't retain the shape you create with it. We'll use a wonderfully easy and fun wire tool that creates a woven tube for *Thetis* (see page 27). You'll learn my trick for adding beads without having to weave them into the core element. I'll show you how to crochet wire into different sized cabled stitches in *Arachne* (see page 34). You'll play with wire wrapping and coil making in this chapter too.

I've intentionally made these projects easy to reproduce so you can practice and feel a sense of accomplishment. As we progress, things get a little trickier, so make sure you take it one step at a time . . . or one wrap at a time, as the case may be! That being said, once you feel comfortable, don't be afraid to take a few risks. Sometimes you can discover something wonderful from creative mishaps. Many of my best ideas come from failed experiments!

1

FOUNDATIONS
WRAPPED, CROCHETED AND COILED SHAPING WIRE DESIGNS

GERBERA

I like to doodle; how about you? I'm particularly fond of doodling flowers. I enjoy it the most when I don't have any agenda: just me, a fine-tip marker and a blank page. This design is a study in free-form doodling with wire. You can make flowers or any other shapes you like. The key here is not to get too uptight about every petal being exactly the same. This is a dimensional wire doodle—have fun with it!

Materials

20-gauge silver-plated Artistic Wire in tangerine, ice blue and rose

eleven 6mm silver-plated jump rings

one 10mm silver-plated jump ring

one large silver-plated swivel lobster clasp

two 6mm gray AB Czech rounds

two SWAROVSKI ELEMENTS 8mm Montana blue rounds

two SWAROVSKI ELEMENTS 8mm vintage rose rounds

Tools

flush cutters

round-nose pliers

two pairs of chain-nose pliers

Finished Length: 8"
(20.5cm)

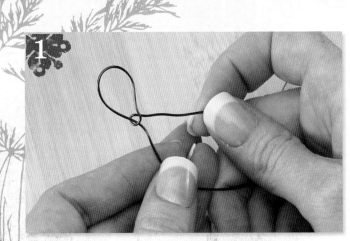

Work from the spool. With 20-gauge orange wire, create a petal approximately 1" (2.5cm) long and 1" (2.5cm) wide at the widest point. Wrap the wire tail around the base of the petal. Use the first petal as a visual guide as you continue.

Make five flower petals, wrapping the wire around the center after forming each one.

Cut the wire, leaving 4" (10cm) of excess. Thread a gray Czech round onto the wire. Wrap the wire around different points in the petals several times.

Cut the wire and tuck both tails under with chain-nose pliers.

Use your fingers to bend the petals into concave shapes to create a dimensional doodle flower.

Repeat Steps 1–5 to make another orange flower, two blue flowers and two pink flowers. Attach Montana blue rounds for the blue flowers and vintage rose rounds for the pink flowers.

Attach the flower petals to create a chain using one 6mm jump ring for each of the two adjacent petals as shown (see *Opening and Closing Jump Rings* on page 14).

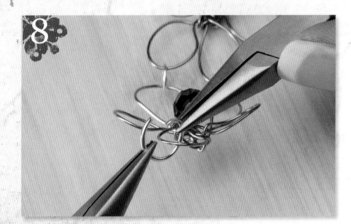

Attach a 10mm jump ring to the outer petal on one end of the bracelet.

Attach a 6mm jump ring and a lobster clasp to the outer petal on the opposite end of the bracelet.

THETIS

Weaving wire on a spool isn't a new idea, but adding beads to the mix can prove complicated and futzy. I figured out a way to create the illusion of spool-woven beads without the frustration of actually having to do it. I love this spool knitter tool because it makes quick work of creating the wire tube. The gold-plated Artistic Wire looks so pretty here, like a sparkly haul from the ocean floor. I flattened this tube, but you can keep it rounded and thread a core strand inside it before you take it off the loom if you like.

Materials

36-gauge gold-plated Artistic Wire

nine SWAROVSKI ELEMENTS 8mm crystal satin rounds

one large silver-plated swivel lobster clasp

six assorted cream buttons

two 6mm silver-plated jump rings

two 12.2mm silver-plated cones

Tools

flush cutters

round-nose pliers

spool knitter tool

two pairs of chain-nose pliers

Finished Length: 18" (45.5cm)

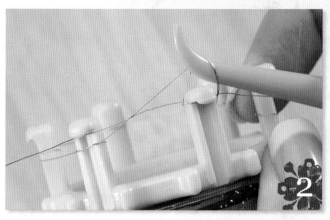

Working from the spool, begin wrapping 36-gauge gold-plated wire around each peg of the spool knitter in a clockwise direction. When you reach the last peg, repeat Step 1. Keep your working wire threaded into the space on the spool where the wire is secured.

Use the hook included with the spool knitter tool to pull the bottom wire over the top wire. This is futzy at first, so be patient.

Twist the spool knitter to move around the pegs faster as you wrap and work. Tug the end of the wire tube through the plastic tube on the spool knitter as you work.

When you have a 17" (43cm) wire tube, remove the wire from the spool. Tie off the ends so they don't unravel.

Flatten the tube by stretching it with your fingers.

Wrap the wire tail at one end of the tube and a 36" (91.5cm) wire segment together.

Begin weaving the 36" (91.5cm) wire segment through the flattened tube. String on a crystal satin round, and then thread the wire back into the tube.

String three crystals onto the left side of the tube, approximately 1" (2.5cm) apart. Attach a cream button in the same manner as the crystals.

Add an assortment of cream buttons and crystals to the front section of the tube, positioning them asymmetrically on the necklace. Add four more crystals to the left side of the tube, approximately 1" (2.5cm) apart.

Thread the wire tail at the end of the tube and the wire segment through a silver-plated cone using chain-nose pliers. Create a wrapped loop with both ends. Repeat on the other side of the tube.

Attach a 6mm jump ring to each wrapped loop and a lobster clasp to one of the jump rings (see *Opening and Closing Jump Rings* on page 14).

VARIATION

This is a more colorful and symmetrical version of the original design. The blue wire is a little bit thicker in diameter, which makes a less delicate tube. I've used fewer crystals here to keep the focus on the knitted wire.

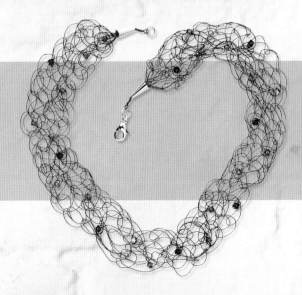

WHIRLIGIG

Our kitchen is painted in the same vibrant colors as this bracelet. It's such fun to wake up in the morning, sit down and have a cup of coffee. I'm not a morning person, so bright colors help perk me up. I am simply mad for the chartreuse wire—how fun is that?! This is a great way to practice wire wrapping, using Quick Links as your base. Practice makes perfect, so let's get to wrapping!

Materials

20-gauge silver-plated wire

24-gauge tangerine Artistic Wire

26-gauge chartreuse Artistic Wire

nine 4mm frosted chartreuse cat's eye glass rondelles

seven 6mm silver-plated jump rings

six 1" (2.5cm) Quick Links

Tools

bench block pad

chasing hammer

flush cutters

steel bench block

two pairs of chain-nose pliers

Finished Length: 7" (18cm)

VARIATION

I wire wrapped small Quick Link circles tightly on one side using the same lovely chartreuse Artistic Wire. Teal wire is loosely wrapped around the vintage plastic oval components. When making earrings, remember to make them in mirror form, so you get a right and a left finished earring.

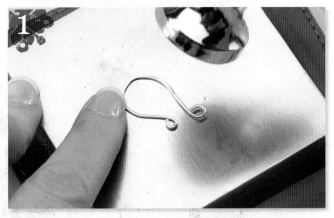

Create a 1" (2.5cm) hammered wire hook using 2½" (6.5cm) of 20-gauge silver-plated wire (see *Creating a Hook and Eye Clasp* on page 16).

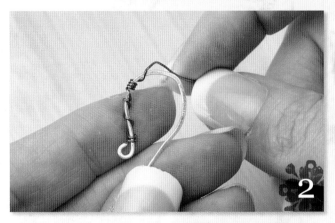

Working from the spool, wrap two tight wraps around the end of the hook with 24-gauge tangerine wire. Continue wrapping the hook in the following pattern: two loose wraps, three tight wraps, two loose wraps, three tight wraps, two loose wraps and two tight wraps at the other end. Cut off the excess wire and tuck in the wire tail.

Wrap a 1" (2.5cm) Quick Link with an 8" (20.5cm) segment of tangerine wire using the following pattern: three tight wraps, two loose wraps. Repeat this pattern four times. End with three tight wraps. Cut off the excess wire and tuck in the wire tail. Repeat with two more Quick Links.

Wrap a Quick Link with 26-gauge chartreuse wire, using the following pattern: four tight wraps, one loose wrap, one loose wrap with a cat's eye rondelle, one loose wrap. Repeat this pattern once. End with four tight wraps. Cut off the excess wire and tuck in the wire tail. The rondelles should face up from the flat edge of the link. Repeat with two more Quick Links.

Attach the wired Quick Links with 6mm jump rings (see *Opening and Closing Jump Rings* on page 14).

Attach the hook to one end of the bracelet with a 6mm jump ring.

BYZANTINE

I was thinking of the puffy turrets on Turkish buildings when I created this ring. I envisioned a round shape graduating upward, knowing full well that this ring would not be an everyday-wear piece, but a more whimsical, on-occasion piece. You could opt for a thicker gauge of wire if you can find beads with larger holes. You can also do a more precise wrap instead of making a wire nest at the ring base. Changing up the little details is how you make a design your own.

Materials

20-gauge peach Artistic Wire

one 10mm fuchsia plastic round

one 20mm orange clear faceted Lucite round

one SWAROVSKI ELEMENTS 8mm mint alabaster round

Tools

chain-nose pliers

chasing hammer

flush cutters

mini anvil

ring mandrel

round-nose pliers

VARIATION

Using similar wire wrapping techniques, I created this cute little button ring. Buttons make fabulous ring components; simply thread your wire tail through the stacked button holes. I added beaded accents and secured them with simple wire loops.

1

2

Working from the spool, string a 20mm orange Lucite round, a 10mm yellow round and an 8mm mint alabaster round onto 20-gauge peach wire. Using round-nose pliers, create a loop in the end of the wire flush to the mint alabaster round.

Wrap the wire around a ring mandrel twice, making the ring one size larger than the desired finished size.

3

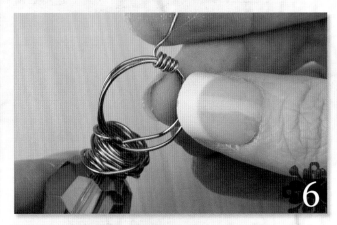

4

Wrap the wire around the base of the orange Lucite bead multiple times, creating a wire nest.

Cut off the excess wire and tuck the tail under the nest.

5

6

Use a mini anvil and chasing hammer to add texture to the ring shank.

Tightly wrap peach wire around the bottom of the ring shank five times. Cut off the excess wire and use chain-nose pliers to tuck the tail flush to the shank.

ARACHNE

I collect bits and pieces from my travels, and I found some lovely antique skeleton keys at a local salvage place I like to haunt. I've slowly used them in a variety of projects, and this crocheted black wire chain was the perfect accompaniment for a wire-wrapped key. This piece is meant to look primitive and imperfect. The open spaces on the wire vary in size and shape, which makes for a striking finished effect.

Materials

18-gauge annealed iron wire

24-gauge black Artistic Wire

one SWAROVSKI ELEMENTS 8mm padparadscha round

one vintage skeleton key

Tools

⅜" (1cm) and ½" (1.5cm) mandrels

5.5mm crochet hook

11.5mm crochet hook

chain-nose pliers

flush cutters

memory wire cutters

round-nose pliers

Finished Length: 20½" (52cm)

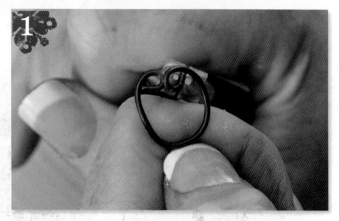

Create a curlicue jump ring by cutting a 2" (5cm) segment of 18-gauge iron wire using memory wire cutters. Make a loop in one end of the iron wire with round-nose pliers. Wrap the wire around a ⅜" (1cm) mandrel to create a circular shape. Cut off ¾" (2cm) of excess wire. Make a matching loop in the other end. The loops should be the same size and flush to one another.

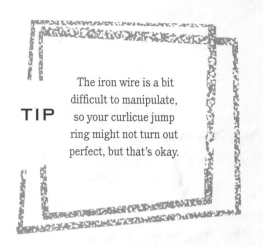

TIP

The iron wire is a bit difficult to manipulate, so your curlicue jump ring might not turn out perfect, but that's okay.

Create a 1" (2.5cm) long wire hook with a 2" (5cm) segment of iron wire. Bend the wire over a ½" (1.5cm) mandrel. Make the second loop facing the same direction as the first loop, so the clasp is shaped like an S. Make a corresponding eye clasp from the iron wire (see *Creating a Hook and Eye Clasp* on page 16).

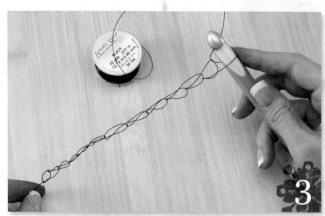

Working from the spool, begin crocheting chain stitches with the 24-gauge black wire. Chain seven stitches with a 5.5mm crochet hook, and then seven stitches with an 11.5mm hook. Repeat this pattern until you have a 19" (48.5cm) segment. Make two more wire chains in the same way.

Tie off the ends of each chain. Use round-nose pliers to coil wrap all three wire ends together.

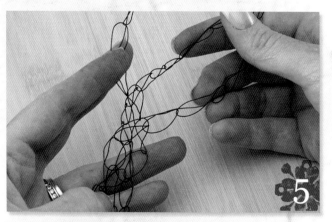

Braid the wires. Use round-nose pliers to coil wrap all three wire ends together on the other end.

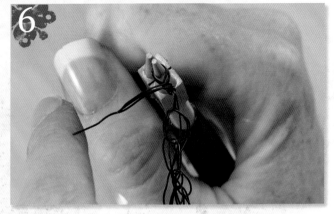

Make a wrapped loop with all three wire ends. Repeat on the other end of the necklace.

Wrap a 2" (5cm) segment of 18-gauge iron wire around the body of a vintage skeleton key five times. Cut off the excess wire and tuck the tail flush to the back of the key.

Wrap the 24-gauge black wire in between the iron wire and string on an 8mm padparadscha round. Cut off the excess wire and tuck the tail flush to the back of the key.

Slide the key into the curlicue jump ring. Attach the jump ring to the center of the braided wire strand.

Attach the hook to the wrapped loop at one end of the necklace. Attach the eye clasp to the other end.

MAGNOLIOPHYTA

I love flowers, but they don't love me. I'm highly allergic to pollen. I brave the outdoors for as long as I can, and when I can't do it anymore, I drape myself with floral-themed accessories and clothing. These lovely Lucite flowers came to life with the addition of brown Artistic Wire stamens and tendrils. I love the unexpected combination of frosted plastic, sparkling crystals and shiny wire. Making the tendrils is so much fun that you might find it a bit addictive. I can't stop looking for ways to integrate them into projects.

Materials

20-gauge brown Artistic Wire

six SWAROVSKI ELEMENTS 6mm light topaz rounds

two 15mm golden yellow Lucite flowers

two 20mm orange Lucite flowers

two 45mm frosted green Lucite 3-petal flowers

two 15mm red Lucite flowers

Tools

12mm mandrel

flush cutters

jump ring maker tool with 4mm mandrel

round-nose pliers

ruler

two pairs of chain-nose pliers

wire cutters

wire rounder tool

Finished Length: 3" (7.5cm) from top of ear wire to bottom stem

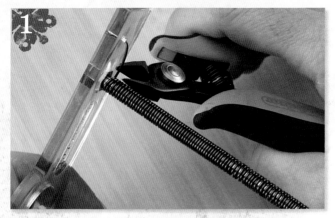

Working from the spool, wrap 20-gauge brown wire tightly around the jump ring maker tool mandrel, working up to the top of the mandrel. Cut the wire from the mandrel.

Remove the coil and gently pull it apart.

Cut the coiled wire into segments of five coils each. These are the wire tendrils.

Use round-nose pliers to form a large loop in one end and a small loop in the other end of each coil segment.

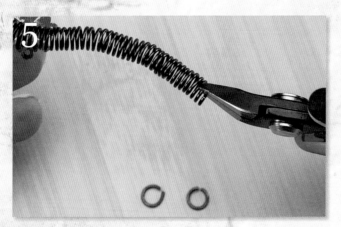

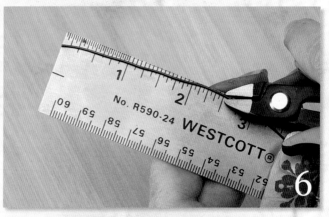

Wrap the wire tightly around the jump ring maker tool mandrel again, working halfway to the center of the mandrel. Make jump rings from this coil (see *Creating Jump Rings* on page 15).

Cut two segments of wire measuring 2½" (6.5cm). Make a large loop in one end of each segment.

Cut a 1¼" (3cm), 1½" (4cm) and 1¾" (4.5cm) segment of wire. Thread a 1¼" (3cm) segment into the top of a red flower and a light topaz round. Use round-nose pliers to make a small loop at the end of the wire and a larger loop at the top of the wire. Thread the 1½" (4cm) wire segment into an orange flower and a light topaz round. Loop both ends as before. Thread the 1¾" (4.5cm) wire segment into a yellow flower and a light topaz round. Loop both ends as before.

Thread the orange flower wire segment and a wire tendril onto a jump ring. Thread a second jump ring with the red flower wire segment and a wire tendril into the first jump ring and secure (see *Opening and Closing Jump Rings* on page 14). Keep the coils on the outside. Thread a third jump ring with the golden yellow flower segment and a wire tendril onto the second jump ring and secure.

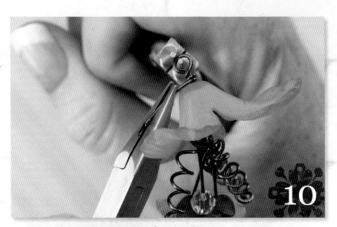

Thread the first jump ring into the large loop on the end of the 2½" (6.5cm) wire segment. Thread this segment into a green flower.

Use round-nose pliers to make a coiled loop flush to the top of the green flower (see *Creating a Coiled Dangle* on page 20). Trim the excess wire. Repeat Steps 7–9 for the second earring.

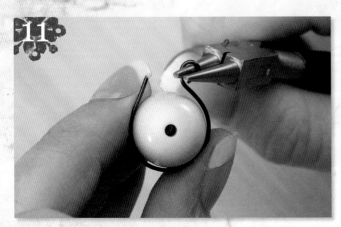

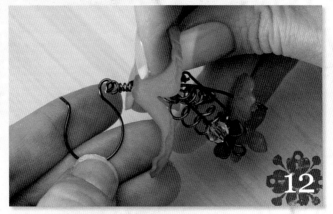

Create two ear wires (see *Creating an Ear Wire* on page 16) from a 1½" (4cm) piece of wire using a 12mm mandrel. I used a 12mm bead. Round the ends of the ear wires.

Attach an ear wire to the loop at the top of each green flower using chain-nose pliers.

Some people can sit and weave small beads and wires into magnificent creations that take endless amounts of patience and concentration. As you might have guessed, I'm not one of them. For me, weaving beading wire using larger beads and making larger dimensional patterns is far more fascinating. In a way, it's like exposing the trick. It's hard to see what's happening in a tiny woven design. I enjoy playing with wire and seeing exactly what it can and cannot do. Each diameter and strand count has new and exciting properties. We're going to create some satisfying projects that will make you start thinking dimensionally. We'll use exposed wire as an element in several ideas and we'll use the wire as a dimensional foundation in others.

Kaleidoscope (see page 45) features several thick sterling silver wires in a gorgeous retro-infused design. By weaving the large beads and wires in a variety of ways, you'll explore some basic woven wire techniques. *Penelope* (see page 50) is inspired by Odysseus' long-suffering wife, who wove and unwove designs while waiting for her husband's return. This piece takes a simple double-needle ladder stitch and adds a new twist for a delightful braided effect. If you like more delicate designs, you'll love *Effervescent* (see page 53). This pretty, open, multi-strand wire idea features circles fashioned from satin silver wire.

Beading wire is more than just the underlying foundation in simple strung designs. It can, with a little imagination, become an important textural and focal element in your work. I suggest starting with inexpensive wire as you test the limits and boundaries. As you become more confident, you can try some of the more exotic wires. Like everything in life, practice makes perfect. You'll find yourself dreaming up new ideas once you've mastered the concepts in this chapter.

2 THINKING IN 3-D
WOVEN BEADING WIRE DESIGNS

BOUGAINVILLEA

This design was inspired by a technique developed by my friend Fernando DaSilva. I made it more formal and symmetrical, and by changing the wire diameter and the bead tension, I got a more stiff and structured result. This technique can easily be adapted to a variety of beads and wires. I was imagining twisting vines and morning glories when I created this.

Materials

7-strand .018" (0.5mm) purple beading wire

20-gauge purple Artistic Wire

eighteen 6mm striated green agate rounds

four 4mm green AB Czech rondelles

four size 1 crimp beads

one 8mm blue plastic flower

one 40mm frosted green Lucite flower

one silver-plated star head pin

twenty 6mm blue cracked Czech glass rounds

two silver-plated Scrimp findings

Tools

bench block pad

chasing hammer

flush cutters

round-nose pliers

two pairs of chain-nose pliers

Scrimp tool

steel bench block

Finished Length: 18" (45.5cm)

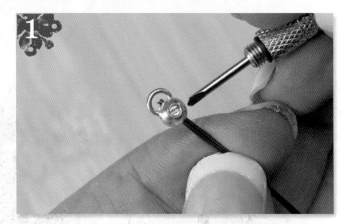

Attach three 20" (51cm) purple beading wires to a Scrimp finding using the Scrimp tool (see *Using a Scrimp* on page 18).

String a blue cracked glass round and a green agate round onto two wires, leaving space between them. Thread the third wire in between the beads and the two core wires. This begins an S-shaped pattern.

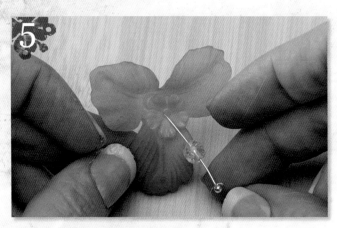

Continue the pattern started in Step 2, sliding beads down as you work to maintain the structure of the design. When you reach the nineteenth blue cracked glass bead, work back through the design and adjust the tension. The S-shaped pattern should be consistent, but don't over-tighten or the design will be too stiff.

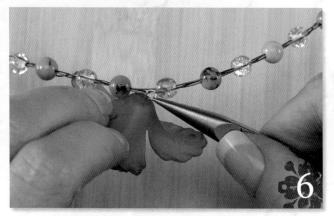

Thread all three wires into a Scrimp, using chain-nose pliers to pull the Scrimp flush to the final bead. Tighten the Scrimp and trim the excess wire.

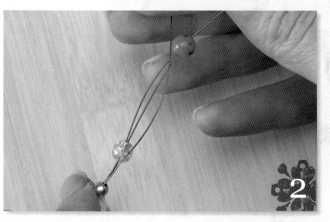

Create a flower by threading a cracked blue glass round, a blue plastic flower and a green Lucite flower onto a star head pin. Make a loop flush against the back of the green flower with round-nose pliers.

Attach the loop at the back of the green flower next to the eleventh bead from the right side of the necklace.

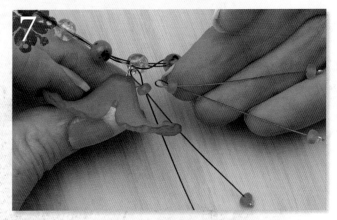

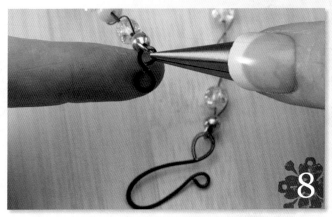

Fold a 6" (15cm) strand of beading wire in half and thread a 4mm green rondelle onto both ends of the wire, pushing it up to form a loop at the top. Add a 4mm green rondelle onto each end of the wire. Secure the ends with a size 1 crimp bead, crimping with chain-nose pliers. Repeat this step once. Attach these components to the loop at the back of the green flower.

Use 20-gauge purple wire to create a hook and eye clasp (see *Creating a Hook and Eye Clasp* on page 16). Hammer the hook flat. Attach the hook to one end of the necklace and the eye clasp to the other end.

VARIATION

These vintage Lucite flower beads lend themselves to lots of lovely jewelry designs. I used beading wire as a base and shaping wire for the tendrils to create this variation on the original design. The concept of wire tendrils is taken in a different direction. I also added some lovely gemstone beads given to me by my aforementioned friend, designer Fernando DaSilva. I'm a fan of the vibrant combination of deep purple and vivid orange. I love the way these colors create such striking contrast!

KALEIDOSCOPE

This is a kaleidoscopic dimensional design that is bursting with personality. I love the kinetic movement in this piece and the combination of a variety of techniques and materials. This necklace can be modified for use with other filigree components—be creative!

Materials

.024" (0.6mm) silver-plated beading wire

22-gauge silver-plated German-style wire

six 10mm yellow Lucite rounds

five 12mm × 14mm transparent hyacinth Lucite barrel beads

four size 3 silver-plated crimp tubes

one 6mm silver-plated jump ring

one 10mm silver-plated jump ring

one silver-plated heart-shaped lobster clasp

nine 12mm × 14mm honey amber quartz Lucite barrel beads

six silver-plated head pins

three 5mm frosted aqua cat's eye glass rondelles

three 10mm × 13mm mustard quartz Lucite oval beads

three 17mm cantaloupe flowers

three 30mm bright tangerine German plastic filigree discs

three 54mm blue zircon German plastic filigree discs

three 13mm translucent orange side-drilled button beads

Tools

flush cutters

Mighty Crimp Tool

round-nose pliers

two pairs of chain-nose pliers

Finished Length: 18" (45.5cm)

Thread a head pin through the back of a blue filigree disc, at the edge of the shape. Thread a cantaloupe flower and an aqua cat's eye rondelle onto the head pin. Make a loop flush against the aqua rondelle to secure the beads.

Thread a head pin through the back of the blue filigree disc, in the center. Thread a tangerine filigree disc and a yellow round onto the head pin. Make a loop flush against the yellow round to secure the beads; they should still be able to move. Repeat Steps 1 and 2 to make two more blue filigree components.

Thread four 23" (58.5cm) silver-plated beading wire segments into a size 3 crimp tube, leaving 1½" (4cm) tails. Crimp with the Mighty Crimp Tool (see *Using a Crimp Tool* on page 17). Trim the excess from two of the wires.

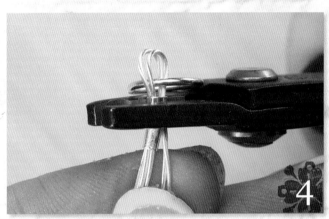

Thread the remaining two wire ends into a second size 3 crimp tube and slide a 10mm jump ring onto the wires. Thread the wires back down through the crimp tube, creating a loop. Crimp and cut off the excess wires.

Thread a honey amber barrel, a hyacinth barrel and another honey amber barrel onto all four wires. Thread a hyacinth barrel onto the first wire, a mustard oval onto the second, a yellow round onto the third and an orange button bead onto the fourth. Thread all four wires into a honey amber barrel, hyacinth barrel and another honey amber barrel.

Thread two wires into a large hole in a blue filigree component, under the center area and into the opposite large hole.

Thread the remaining two wires under the filigree, through the same large hole, over the center and into the opposite large hole, coming out under the edge of the filigree.

Thread all four wires into a honey amber barrel bead. Repeat Steps 6 and 7 with the remaining two blue filigree components, threading a honey amber barrel bead onto all four wires after each one.

Thread a hyacinth barrel onto the first wire, a mustard oval onto the second, a yellow round onto the third and an orange button bead onto the fourth. Thread a honey amber barrel onto all four wires. Repeat this pattern once more. Adjust your wires. Don't use too much tension, or the design will be stiff.

Thread all four wires into a size 3 crimp tube and crimp. Cut two of the wires flush to the tube. Thread the remaining two wire ends into a second size 3 crimp tube and slide a 6mm jump ring with a lobster clasp attached to it onto the wires. Thread the wires back down through the crimp tube, creating a loop. Crimp and cut off the excess wires.

Use 22-gauge German-style wire to conceal the crimp tubes, wrapping over them in a free-form manner. Cut off the excess wire and tuck in the tails with chain-nose pliers.

CIRCE

The wires in this bracelet are an integral element in the design. They wrap in and out of beautiful beads, creating tension. Using delicate beads gives this bracelet a stiffness that's reminiscent of a bangle. A single steampunk stone bead adds the perfect touch of movement. Try this technique with different wires and beads for a multitude of effects.

Materials

7-strand .018" (0.5mm) red beading wire

four 5mm hematite rice beads

four 7mm gray AB Czech faceted tubes

one Earthenwood steampunk stone

one silver-plated swivel lobster clasp

seven 4mm faceted hematite rounds

two 6mm silver-plated jump rings

two silver-plated Scrimp ends

Tools

Scrimp tool

two pairs of chain-nose pliers

wire cutters

Finished Length: 7" (18cm)

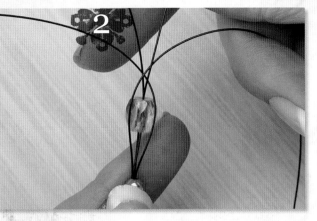

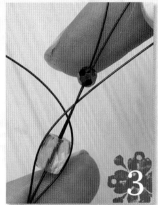

Attach four 8" (20.5cm) segments of red beading wire to a Scrimp finding with a Scrimp tool (see *Using a Scrimp* on page 18). Thread the center two wires into a gray faceted tube.

Thread the remaining two wires around the tube and criss-cross them between the two center wires.

String a faceted hematite round onto the center wires. Repeat the criss-cross pattern from Step 2. Slide the beads down to the end of the work to create tension. If the weave is too loose, the design won't work.

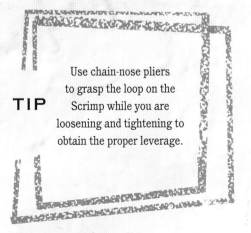

Thread a hematite rice bead onto the center wires and weave as before. Thread a faceted hematite onto the center wires and weave. Continue with the established pattern from Steps 2–4, creating tension as you progress. Stop after the fourth hematite rice bead.

Slide all four wires into a Scrimp end. Use chain-nose pliers to pull the wires through. Tighten the finding.

Attach a 6mm jump ring to one Scrimp end and a second jump ring with a steampunk stone and a lobster clasp to the opposite end (see *Opening and Closing Jump Rings* on page 14). Test the Scrimps to ensure they are properly secured.

TIP Use chain-nose pliers to grasp the loop on the Scrimp while you are loosening and tightening to obtain the proper leverage.

PENELOPE

This sumptuous woven bracelet is an explosion of color moving sinuously around your wrist. A simple double-needle ladder stitch is interwoven to create a dimensional design that can be adapted for a variety of bead sizes. Rounds work best for this concept, though bicones or ovals could be substituted. Just remember that the core strand must be at least an inch (2.5cm) longer than the desired finished bracelet.

Materials

49-strand .018" (0.5mm) beading wire

fifty-three SWAROVSKI ELEMENTS 8mm fuchsia rounds

fifty-three SWAROVSKI ELEMENTS 8mm Indian red rounds

fifty-three SWAROVSKI ELEMENTS 8mm padparadscha rounds

one silver-plated three-strand slide clasp

six size 3 silver-plated crimp tubes

Tools

Mighty Crimp Tool

chain-nose pliers

ruler

Finished Length: 8" (20.5cm) to fit a 7" (18cm) wrist

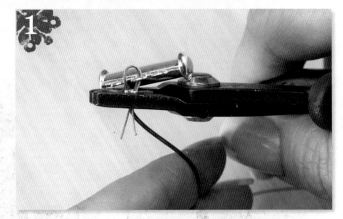

Thread two 12" (30.5cm) segments of beading wire through a size 3 crimp tube and the center loop of a three-strand slide clasp, and then back through the crimp tube. Crimp with the Mighty Crimp Tool (see *Using a Crimp Tool* on page 17). Cut off the excess wire.

Thread four fuchsia rounds onto the left wire and five fuchsia rounds onto the right wire. Thread the left wire through the fifth fuchsia round on the right wire, going in the opposite direction. Pull the wires to create an oval shape.

Repeat Step 2 to make four more ovals. When you reach the fifth oval, thread four beads onto each wire. Thread both wires into a crimp tube, through the center loop on the other half of the slide clasp, and back through the crimp tube. Use chain-nose pliers to grasp and pull the wires through the tube. Make sure the design is neither too tight nor too loose before you crimp. If you don't allow for some "play" between the beads, the bracelet will be too stiff to wear. Try rounding it before crimping to ensure flexibility.

Attach two 13" (33cm) beading wires to the left loop on the three-strand slide clasp using a crimp tube (see Step 1). Cut off the excess wire. Thread four Indian red rounds on the outer wire. Thread the inner wire under and through the first oval in the center strand. Thread a fifth bead on the inner wire, and then thread the outer wire through the fifth bead in the opposite direction. Pull the wires to create an oval.

Repeat Step 4, continuing to thread crystals on both wires and threading the inner wire up through the corresponding oval in the center strand. When you reach the sixth oval of Indian red rounds, thread the wires into a crimp tube, through the left loop on the other half of the slide clasp, and then back through the crimp tube. Use chain-nose pliers to grasp and pull the wires through the tube. Crimp and cut off the excess wire.

Attach two 13" (33cm) wires to the right loop on the slide clasp. Repeat the process in Steps 4 and 5 using padparadscha rounds. When you reach the sixth oval of padparadscha rounds, thread the wires into a crimp tube, through the left loop on the other half of the slide clasp, and then back through the crimp tube. Use chain-nose pliers to grasp and pull the wires through the tube. Crimp and cut off the excess wire. Check all crimp tubes to be sure they're properly closed.

TIP

If your wrist is larger, try adding another oval to each strand of crystals. Remember that the center strand needs to be an inch longer than the desired length of the bracelet.

VARIATION

I made the same bracelet using different colors and bead shapes. If you change your beads, you'll need to adjust the measurements. Cool colors and the combination of gemstone, cat's eye glass and SWAROVSKI ELEMENTS with varied opacities make a fascinating combination.

EFFERVESCENT

Beading wire circles can be created using a variety of techniques. I've been playing around with this for a few years now. This necklace features wire lengths that are stationed by a bead and two crimp beads, creating permanently rounded forms. These little circles can be varied in size and shape, or cut from the base wire and used as dangling elements. You can also bead the circumference of each circle before securing it. Different diameters of wire will result in more or less flexible circles. I love the light and bubbly feeling this necklace evokes. It reminds me of my favorite beverage, champagne; thus I named it *Effervescent!*

Materials

7-strand .018" (0.5mm) satin silver beading wire

one silver-plated heart-shaped lobster clasp

one small silver-plated toggle ring

six silver-plated loop crimp ends

twelve SWAROVSKI ELEMENTS 8mm crystal satin rounds

twelve SWAROVSKI ELEMENTS 8mm pacific green opal rounds

twenty-four size 2 silver-plated crimp tubes

two 6mm silver-plated jump rings

Tools

flush cutters

ruler

two pairs of chain-nose pliers

Finished Length: 19½" (49.5cm)

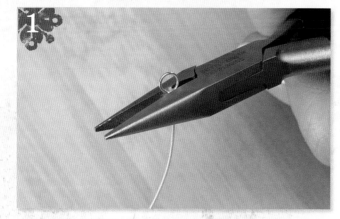

Attach three 3" (7.5cm) satin silver beading wires to three loop crimp ends using chain-nose pliers. Test each crimp to be sure the wire is secured.

Thread a size 2 crimp tube, a crystal satin round and a second crimp tube onto one of the wires (see *Making Beading Wire Circles* on page 21). Form the wire into a 1" (2.5cm) diameter circle and thread it back into the tube, the bead and the second tube. The circle should be 2" (5cm) from the end of the wire.

TIP You must use a lot of pressure to attach the loop crimp ends securely.

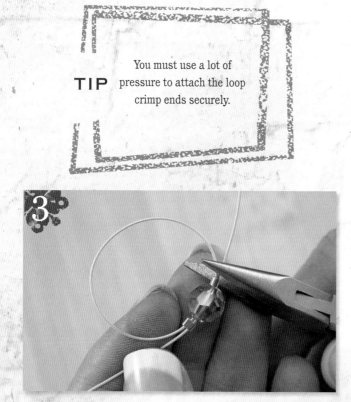

Grasp the circle with your fingers. Use chain-nose pliers to secure the crimps flush to each side of the bead.

Make a second wire circle 1½" (4cm) from the first circle, using the same process as in Steps 2 and 3, using a pacific green opal round. Alternate between satin and green crystals, spacing each one 1½" (4cm) apart and stopping after the eighth circle.

TIP Use chain-nose pliers to crimp the tubes for illusion designs such as this one, so that the circles maintain their shapes.

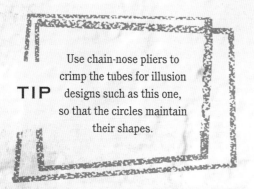

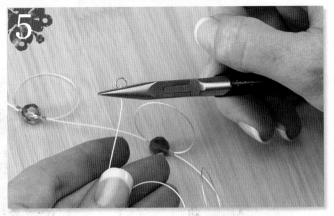

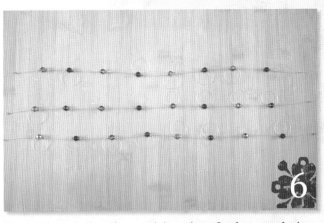

Trim the wire, leaving 2" (5cm) of wire after the last circle. Thread the wire end into a loop crimp and secure it with chain-nose pliers.

Repeat Steps 2–5 on the remaining wires. On the second wire, begin the first circle 2¼" (5.5cm) from the loop crimp and cut the wire 2¼" (5.5cm) after the last circle. On the third wire, begin the first circle 2¾" (7cm) from the loop crimp and cut the wire 2¾" (7cm) after the last circle. The finished wires should be approximately 18½" (47cm), 19" (48.5cm) and 20" (51cm).

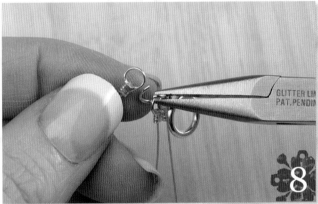

Attach all three finished strands to a 6mm jump ring and a lobster clasp (see *Opening and Closing Jump Rings* on page 14).

Attach all three finished strands on the opposite end to a 6mm jump ring and a small toggle ring.

VARIATION

These earrings were created to coordinate with the necklace. Rather than build the circles on a wire base, I cut the wire ends from each side. A small chain segment adds texture and movement. Simply fabulous.

DIAGONAL

I've been playing with exposed wire designs for over ten years. It's amazing how many directions you can take a few wires and beads if you're willing to experiment. I love how this three-strand design creates a center zigzag pattern between the larger white alabaster crystals. When I'm working on these concepts, I keep throwing beads on the wire in a variety of patterns until something emerges. It's very intuitive, which is how some of the best designs are created.

Materials

7-strand .018" (0.5mm) black beading wire

four 6mm silver-plated jump rings

nineteen SWAROVSKI ELEMENTS 8mm white alabaster rounds

one sterling silver toggle clasp

ten SWAROVSKI ELEMENTS 4mm crystal copper rounds

ten SWAROVSKI ELEMENTS 4mm indicolite rounds

ten SWAROVSKI ELEMENTS 4mm jet AB rounds

ten SWAROVSKI ELEMENTS 4mm jonquil rounds

two 6mm silver-plated jump rings

two size 4 silver-plated or sterling crimp tubes

Tools

flush cutters

Mighty Crimp Tool

two pairs of chain-nose pliers

Finished Length: 16½" (42cm)

Cut three 20" (51cm) segments of black beading wire. Thread a size 4 crimp tube onto all three wires. Thread the wires onto a 6mm jump ring attached to a toggle ring (see *Opening and Closing Jump Rings* on page 14). Thread the wires back into the tube. Use chain-nose pliers to pull the wires through. Crimp and cut the excess wire flush to the bottom of the crimp tube (see *Using a Crimp Tool* on page 17).

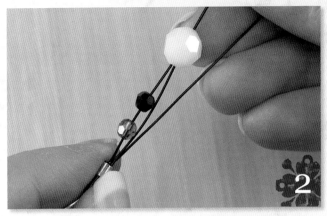

Thread a crystal copper round and a jet round onto the left wire. Thread a white alabaster round onto the left and the center wires.

Thread a jonquil round and an indicolite round onto the center wire. Thread a white alabaster round onto the center and right wires.

Thread a crystal copper round and a jet round onto the center wire. Thread a white alabaster round onto the left and center wires.

Repeat Steps 3 and 4 until you use the eighteenth white alabaster bead. Thread a crystal copper round and a jet round onto the right wire. Thread a white alabaster bead onto the center and left wires. Thread a jonquil round and an indicolite round onto the left wire. The outer wires will have a slight curvature, but too much curve means your tension is too tight. Adjust the tension if necessary.

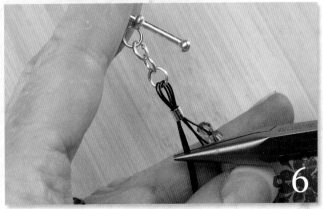

Thread all three wires into a crimp tube. Thread the wires onto a 6mm jump ring attached to two more jump rings and a toggle bar. Thread the wires back into the tube. Use chain-nose pliers to pull the wires through. Crimp and cut the excess wire flush to the bottom of the crimp tube.

So you've mastered the basics of shaping wire, you've played with some tools and techniques and you're feeling confident enough to take on some new challenges. Good for you! This chapter is going to take what you've learned a step further. I'm a big fan of designs that look complex, but are, in fact, not too difficult to recreate. I like organic, dimensional, simple and striking jewelry. This is a chapter full of those sorts of designs. They will require more patience, more effort and more time, but you will be rewarded with jewelry that captures attention while still complementing the wearer. Try these ideas out with a variety of wires and see how the outcome changes. Every material, every finish and every gauge will result in a unique result—that's the fun of it!

Helix (see page 60) uses simple copper wire and a jump ring maker tool to create a chain from scratch. You'll use wire and beads to make fascinating spiral shapes you can connect together. *Lepidoptera* (see page 69) is a simply stunning butterfly choker made of copper wire that has been formed on a wire jig, hammered and wrapped into organic shapes. It is accented with a stunning ocean blue SWAROVSKI ELEMENTS teardrop dangle. *Atlantis* (see page 74) is perhaps my favorite design in the book (though, truth be told, they're all my favorites for different reasons). This piece is absolutely gorgeous when worn, like an haute couture necklace with a decidedly bohemian flair.

Once you've worked your way through this chapter, you will have developed a very good feel for the potential of shaping wire. Still, we've only scratched the surface. There are a variety of aesthetics currently being explored in wireworking, from the simple and organic ideas I embrace to more complex wrapped and woven designs other artists prefer. Don't stop here—keep expanding outward, and as you expand, explore and experiment until you find the style that suits you best.

3 SCULPTURAL CONCEPTS
COMPLEX DIMENSIONAL SHAPING WIRE AND BEAD DESIGNS

HELIX

I started playing with wire coils in my last book. Like many techniques, they become obsessions. Here, I added dimension with wire and beads and threaded core beads into the center, which really turned out to be interesting stuff. I know I may start to sound like a broken record, but don't be afraid to play with this idea. See where you can take it. Add your own little twists and turns—that's what makes designing so much fun!

Materials

20-gauge copper Artistic Wire

24-gauge gunmetal Artistic Wire

eighteen 6mm faceted hematite bicones

three 6mm copper jump rings

twenty-five 4mm faceted hematite rounds

Tools

bench block pad

chasing hammer

jump ring maker tool with 8mm and 15mm dowel

round-nose pliers

steel bench block

two pairs of chain-nose pliers

Finished Length: 18½" (47cm)

Thread 20-gauge copper wire into the hole on the jump ring maker tool. Wrap the wire 2" (5cm) up the 15mm dowel.

Remove the coil and cut it into three 1½" (4cm) segments. There will be about three coils in each segment.

Use round-nose pliers to create loops on each side of each coil segment as shown.

Starting after the loop, wrap 24-gauge gunmetal wire five times around the end of one of the coils (see *Shaping and Hammering Wire* on page 14).

Thread a 4mm faceted hematite round onto the 24-gauge wire, and then wrap five more times. Cut the wire tail and tuck it in with chain-nose pliers. Repeat Steps 4 and 5 along the entire coil, spacing each wrapped and beaded segment about ³⁄₁₆" (5mm) apart.The number of segments will depend on how separated the coils are; this is something you'll need to adjust as you work. Make two more completely wrapped coils.

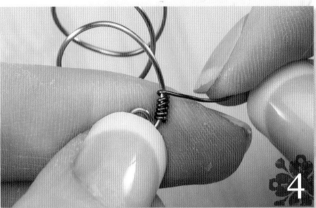

Cut a 5" (12.5cm) piece of 20-gauge wire. Make a loop in one end. Thread this wire through the left loop on one of the coils. Thread six 6mm faceted hematite bicones onto the 20-gauge wire.

Thread the end of the 20-gauge wire segment through the right loop in the coil. Create a second loop flush to the coil loop with round-nose pliers. Give the interior of the coil a slight bend with your fingers. Repeat Steps 6 and 7 with the remaining coils. Attach the beaded coils with manufactured 6mm copper jump rings (see *Opening and Closing Jump Rings* on page 14).

Using 20-gauge wire and a jump ring maker tool with an 8mm dowel, make eighty-eight jump rings (see *Creating Jump Rings* on page 15). Use these jump rings to build the necklace chain. Make two sets of three connected jump rings. Connect these segments with a single jump ring at the top.

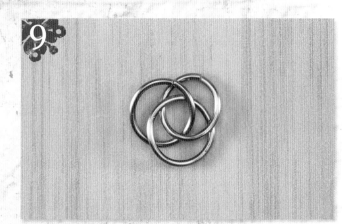

Make a "flower" chain segment from three jump rings as shown. Connect the single jump ring from Step 8 through all three jump rings in the "flower" chain segment.

Make two more sets of three connected jump rings. Connect these sets to all three jump rings in the "flower" chain segment as shown. Continue in the following pattern: single jump ring, flower chain segment, two three-jump-ring segments. Stop after the fifth single jump ring. Make an identical chain for the opposite side of the necklace.

Attach the chains to either side of the coil components from Step 7.

Create a hammered hook from 20-gauge copper wire and attach it to the final link on the right side of the necklace chain (see *Creating a Hook and Eye Clasp* on page 16).

BQOTU

You too can crown yourself Bead Queen of the Universe. First, you must muster up as much moxie, chutzpah and unmitigated gall as possible, and then you must patiently and methodically wrap a wire tiara base with a gazillion tiny crystal beads. You will wrap and wrap and wrap . . . and then you will wrap some more. This project is all about tension. Too little and the tiara will be floppy; too much and it might break. As you practice wrapping and twisting wire and crystals, you will find the perfect balance, and your tiara will be beautiful—just like you, bead queen.

Materials

24-gauge silver-plated German-style wire

forty-five SWAROVSKI ELEMENTS 8mm crystal AB faceted rounds

one metal tiara base

two hundred forty-one SWAROVSKI ELEMENTS 4mm crystal AB rounds

Tools

chain-nose pliers

wire cutters

63

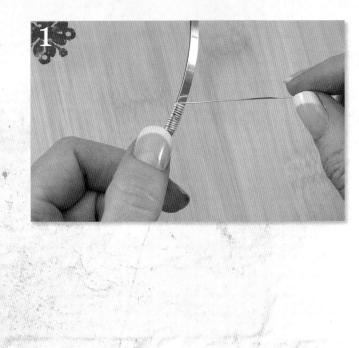

Remove as much 24-gauge German-style wire from the spool as you can use comfortably, without too much kinking. I used about a 4' (122cm) long segment. You will run out of wire before you finish; when you reach the end of one piece, tuck it flush to the back of the tiara base and patch in a new wire. I used two 4' (122cm) wire segments to make this tiara. Wrap the wire around the metal tiara base, starting 2½" (6.5cm) from the end. Wrap the wire tightly around the base thirteen times.

Thread an 8mm crystal onto the wire, and then wrap the wire around the tiara base three times.

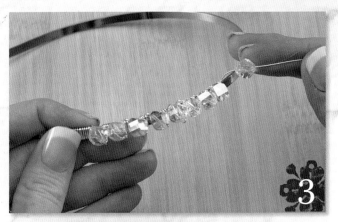

Thread another 8mm crystal onto the wire, and then wrap the wire around the tiara base three times. Continue adding 8mm crystals in this manner until you reach the ninth crystal.

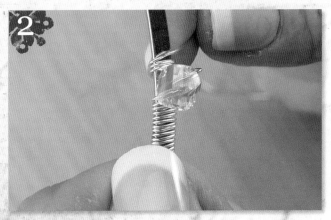

Thread the wire with seven 4mm crystals, one 8mm crystal and seven more 4mm crystals. Wrap the wire around the base two times.

Grasp the bottom of the loop and twist it twice to secure it and create tension.

Thread an 8mm crystal onto the wire, flush to the front of the loop. Wrap the wire two times. Bring the wire up and around the back of the bead and wrap it around the base one more time.

Repeat Steps 4–6 to make loops with the following crystal counts: eight 4mm/one 8mm/eight 4mm; nine 4mm/one 8mm/nine 4mm; nine 4mm/one 8mm/nine 4mm; ten 4mm/one 8mm/ten 4mm; eleven 4mm/one 8mm/eleven 4mm; twelve 4mm/one 8mm/twelve 4mm; and thirteen 4mm/one 8mm/ thirteen 4mm as your center loop. After making each loop, wrap an 8mm crystal flush to the front of the loop, as in Step 6. After the center loop, continue the pattern in reverse, ending with a seven 4mm/one 8mm/seven 4mm loop.

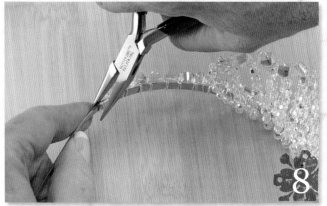

Wrap the wire around the base three times. Begin wrapping 8mm crystals around the tiara as in Step 3. Stop after the ninth crystal, and finish with thirteen wire wraps. Cut off the excess wire and use chain-nose pliers to secure the wire tail flush to the back of the tiara base.

VARIATION

If you're not a tiara kind of gal, a wire-wrapped headband is a nice alternative. Here, I've used the same tiara base and wrapped it with reconstituted turquoise rounds. I created a bead and wire flower with some chrysocolla teardrop beads.

DRAGONMOON

I have always been fascinated by dragonflies. The dragonfly has become a recurring motif in my work, and this incarnation has a decidedly Asian feel. Designing the pattern was an organic experience. I wanted to use the coral beads, but I wanted them to be away from the neck, where they might prove scratchy. So I wrapped a second wire around the beaded core and added blue glass rondelles to create a wave-like effect. As I wrapped, I began to visualize a dragon's tail. When I reached the end, I knew I had to make a little dragonfly to conceal the clasp and give this design a sculptural feel.

Materials

18-gauge non-tarnish silver-plated Artistic Wire

24-gauge silver-plated German-style wire

one 8mm citrus green moonglow Lucite round

one hundred fifteen 4mm pea green opaque Czech glass rondelles

one hundred one 4mm light topaz blue translucent Czech glass rondelles

one hundred thirty-three small red coral fringes

Tools

anvil or steel bench block

bench block pad

chain-nose pliers

chasing hammer

round-nose pliers

wire cutters

Finished length: 16"
(40.5cm)

Cut a 20" (51cm) segment of 18-gauge non-tarnish silver-plated wire. Make a loop in one end. Slide on 114 green rondelles. Make a second loop in the end to secure the beads.

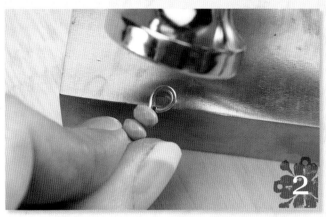

Use a chasing hammer and an anvil or a steel bench block to hammer the loops at each end of the beaded segment. Make a hammered hook from 1½" (4cm) of 18-gauge wire and set it aside (see *Creating a Hook and Eye Clasp* on page 16).

Cut a 4' (122cm) piece of 24-gauge German-style wire. Wrap this wire tightly between the loop and the first green bead. String on five red coral fringes and four blue rondelles. Wrap the wire tightly around the base between the sixth and seventh green rondelles. Continue stringing coral and blue beads onto the 24-gauge wire and wrapping between every sixth and seventh green rondelle on the core wire. There should be six green rondelles between each wrap. When you reach the final beaded segment, secure the wire tightly around the end of the core wire. Cut off the excess wire and tuck in the tail.

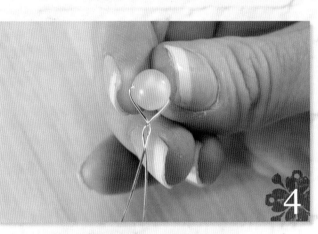

Create the dragonfly by cutting a 16" (40.5cm) segment of 24-gauge German-style wire. Slide a green moonglow round onto the center of the wire. Bend the wire flush to each side of the green moonglow round. Grasp the bead between your thumb and forefinger and hold the bottoms of the wire tails in your opposite hand. Twist the bead one time.

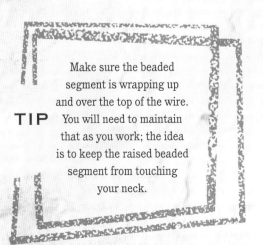

TIP Make sure the beaded segment is wrapping up and over the top of the wire. You will need to maintain that as you work; the idea is to keep the raised beaded segment from touching your neck.

Thread eighteen red coral fringes onto each wire tail, followed by eight blue rondelles. Wrap each wire tail around and over the top of the opposite wire tail as shown, creating wings.

String one wire end with nine blue rondelles. Wrap the wire end around this beaded tail, after the fourth bead and seventh bead from the bottom. Cut off the excess and tuck the wire into the underside of the tail.

Use the other wire to securely wrap the dragonfly to the end of the core necklace.

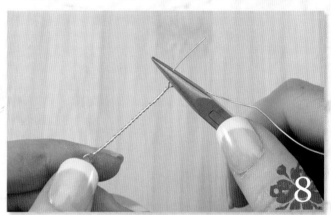

Cut a 14" (35.5cm) segment of wire. Thread a blue rondelle onto the wire, 1½" (4cm) from the end. Fold the wire over the bead and grasp the bead between your thumb and forefinger. Twist the wires together, holding the wire ends securely with chain-nose pliers.

Repeat Step 8 two more times; each twisted segment should be slightly longer than the last. Gently curve the twisted wires as shown.

Attach the twisted segments to the core wire, beneath the dragonfly. Cut off the excess wire and tuck the tail under with chain-nose pliers. Attach the hammered hook from Step 2 to the opposite end of the core wire.

This design was born while playing with a wire jig. When placed back-to-back, the two curved shapes immediately evoked butterfly wings. My job was to keep the design simple and organic. I find that the more I progress as a designer, the more simplicity in form excites me.

Materials

18-gauge natural copper Artistic Wire

20-gauge natural copper Artistic Wire

one SWAROVSKI ELEMENTS 12mm × 25mm ocean blue flat teardrop

three 6mm copper jump rings

Tools

bench block pad

chasing hammer

flush cutters

jump ring maker tool with 12mm dowel

nylon jaw pliers

round-nose pliers

steel bench block

Thing-A-Ma-Jig tool

two pairs of chain-nose pliers

Finished Length: 20" (51cm)

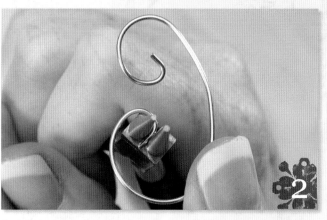

Wrap a 6" (15cm) piece of 18-gauge copper wire around the two pegs on a Thing-A-Ma-Jig tool as shown. Cut off the excess wire tail.

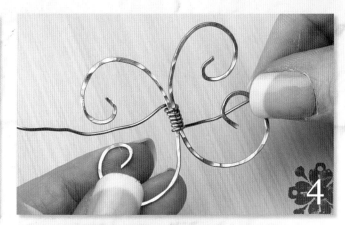

Curl the wire ends into spirals as shown, using the largest part of the jaw of round-nose pliers.

Make six of these shapes, with three facing to the left and three facing to the right. Hammer each shape to flatten and add texture.

Connect a left- and right-facing shape into a butterfly by wrapping them with 20-gauge copper wire. Wrap eight times around the center of the two shapes, binding them together. Cut off the excess wire and tuck in the tail. Use chain-nose pliers to compress the coils.

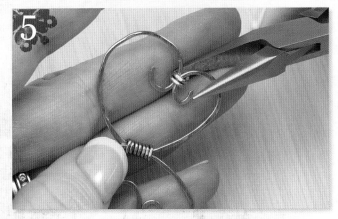

Wrap the outer edges of each spiral with 20-gauge wire, wrapping two times on each side. Compress the coils as before.

Attach the butterflies together at the top parts of the wings using manufactured 6mm jump rings (see *Opening and Closing Jump Rings* on page 14).

Use the jump ring maker tool to create twenty-seven 12mm jump rings with the 18-gauge copper wire (see *Creating Jump Rings* on page 15). Flatten the rings on the steel bench block with the flat side of the chasing hammer. Link the jump rings into a simple chain.

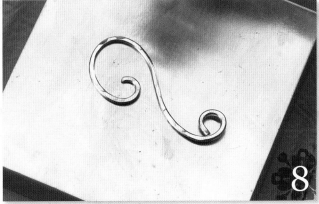

Using 18-gauge copper wire, create a 1¾" (4.5cm) fancy hook as shown (see *Creating a Hook and Eye Clasp* on page 16). Flatten the hook with the chasing hammer and steel bench block.

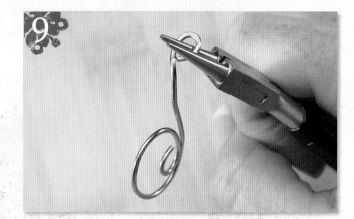

Using 18-gauge copper wire, create a 1½" (4cm) spiral-ended hook as shown. Start by loosely flat-coiling the end of a 3" (7.5cm) wire segment using round-nose pliers and nylon jaw pliers. Hammer the shape. Make a loop perpendicular to the front of the shape with round-nose pliers.

Thread a 4" (10cm) segment of 20-gauge wire into the drill hole in an ocean blue flat teardrop. Coil one end of the wire to make a bail and cut off any excess. Wrap the other end around the top of the pendant in a free-form manner with tension. When you reach the end of the wire, use round-nose pliers to create a loop in the wire end.

Attach the teardrop dangle to the spiral-ended hook by sliding it onto the coiled end.

Attach the spiral-ended hook to the butterfly.

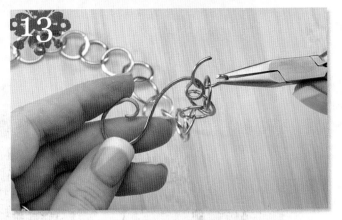

Attach the fancy hook to one end of the simple chain.

Connect the simple chain to the outside wing of the left butterfly.

TIP

Copper will oxidize fairly quickly. You can clean it if you choose. Or, if you prefer the oxidized look, there are a variety of chemicals you can buy at the hardware store, such as liver of sulfur, muriatic acid solution and cupric nitrate solution, to speed that process along and make it permanent.

VARIATION

This bracelet uses similar shapes created on a jig, in an S-pattern instead of a C-curve. I wired two shapes together using 24-gauge German-style silver-plated wire and added beads to conceal the wire wraps and give the design some dimension. The bracelet mechanism is created by wrapping a flat-hammered 18-gauge copper wire around a round shape that is about the same size as the wearer's wrist. Use round-nose pliers to make a loop on one side and a hook that connects into the outer curve at the top of the bracelet.

ATLANTIS

I began with the idea of hammered, wired, flat half-circles that created a scale-like effect as they cascaded from the neck. My initial vision was all metal, but as I began to problem solve, I realized that a beading wire base with pretty blue beads would create a fabulous foundation for the links. Then, I started thinking on a larger scale and added beaded accents to mimic the half-circle motif. Finally, I added swingy beads at the bottom of each half-circle to give the design some movement and interest. I tried on the finished piece and gasped. Wow. I felt like a mer-queen!

Materials

18-gauge gunmetal Artistic Wire

49-strand .018" (0.5mm) beading wire

one gunmetal spring ring clasp

one hundred twenty-nine 7mm × 8mm aquatic blue AB Czech glass pillow beads

sixteen size 2 gunmetal crimp beads

thirty-six 1½" (4cm) gunmetal head pins

two 8mm gunmetal jump rings

Tools

2" (5cm) mandrel (optional)

bench block pad

chasing hammer

flush cutters

round-nose pliers

standard crimp tool

steel bench block

two pairs of chain-nose pliers

Finished Length: 16" (40.5cm)

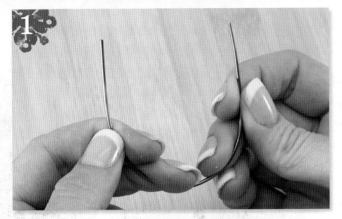

Cut a 5½" (14cm) segment of 18-gauge gunmetal wire. Wrap the wire around a 2" (5cm) mandrel or free-form wrap to create a half-circle shape as shown. The opening should be 2" (5cm) wide. Make thirteen half-circles.

Use round-nose pliers to form loops at the top of each half-circle. The loops should face toward the back of the circle as shown.

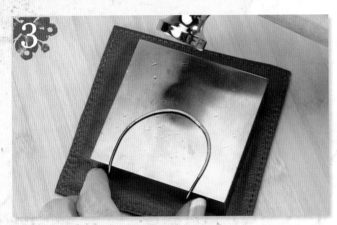

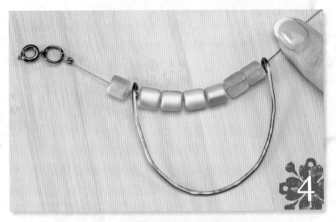

Hammer the curved portion of each half-circle flat. Use the round end of the chasing hammer to add texture to the front of each half-circle.

Thread an 18" (45.5cm) segment of beading wire through a size 2 crimp bead and an 8mm jump ring with a spring ring clasp attached, and then back through the crimp bead. Crimp with a standard crimp tool. (see *Using a Crimp Tool* on page 17). Trim the excess wire. String on a blue pillow bead, one end of a half-circle, six more blue pillow beads and the other end of the half-circle.

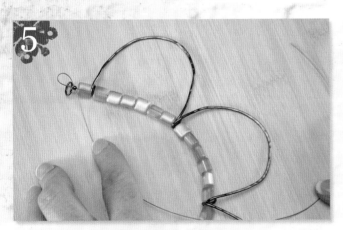

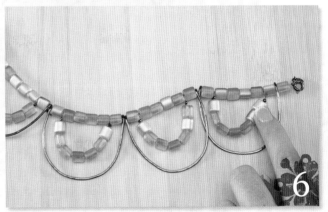

String on five more half-circles with six pillow beads inside each. Add a final blue pillow bead and attach the wire to an 8mm jump ring using a crimp bead. Leave some play between the beads by rounding the design before you crimp. Trim the excess wire.

Attach a 4" (10cm) segment of wire to the core necklace with a crimp bead and chain-nose pliers, positioning it within the first half-circle, after the first bead. String seven beads onto this wire, and then attach the end to the core necklace before the last bead within the first half-circle. Repeat this process, adding beaded half circles inside each wire half-circle.

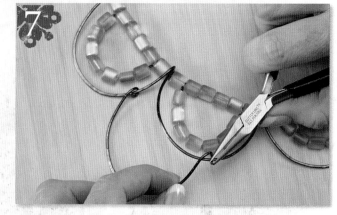

Attach a second row of six wire half-circles to the bottom of every two half-circles in the top row.

Create thirty-six loop-top dangles (see *Creating a Loop-Top Dangle* on page 21). Slide a blue pillow bead onto a head pin and make a loop using round-nose pliers flush to the top of the bead. Trim the excess wire.

Attach six loop-top dangles to each half-circle in the second row of the necklace.

VARIATION

My lovely and talented daughter Avalon has been sculpturally driven since she picked up her first set of blocks. She asked to create the variation for this project, and her necklace and earrings blew me away! Instead of beaded swags and dangling beads, she created a simple beaded foundation and added three layers of brass wire half-circles. This design makes me think of dragon scales. As you can see, a basic concept can be taken in infinite directions.

AMPHORA

18-gauge brass wire is hammered, shaped and wrapped to create this ancient-looking work of wearable art. I found these uniquely colored cucumber green cat's eye glass pillow beads, and I love the way they work with garnet red. This project lets you build a design using a variety of techniques that you can adapt to create your own unique work of art.

Materials

18-gauge non-tarnish brass Artistic Wire

22-gauge non-tarnish brass Artistic Wire

34-gauge non-tarnish brass Artistic Wire

eighteen gold-plated head pins

fifteen 3mm red garnet glass round beads

nine 6mm faceted black Czech glass beads

six 6mm gold-plated jump rings

twelve 7mm cucumber green cat's eye glass pillow beads

Tools

1½" (4cm) mandrel

bench block pad

chasing hammer

flush cutters

jump ring maker tool with a 16mm dowel

memory wire cutters

rat tail comb or other thin metal dowel

round-nose pliers

steel bench block

two pairs of chain-nose pliers

Finished Length: 18" (45.5cm)

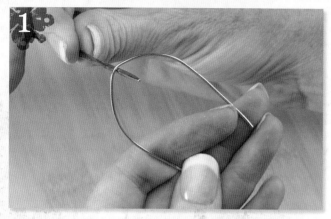

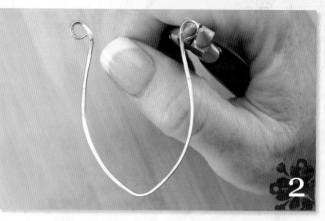

Create the focal element by bending a 5" (12.5cm) segment of 18-gauge non-tarnish brass wire around a 1½" (4cm) round dowel (I used a spool of thread.) Use a rat tail comb or other thin metal dowel to create a bend in the center of the wire. Hammer the shape flat (see *Shaping and Hammering Wire* on page 14).

Use round-nose pliers to bend the top ends into loops as shown.

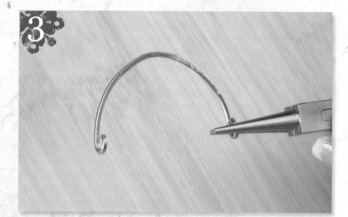

Bend a 2½" (6.5cm) segment of wire around a 1½" (4cm) round dowel. Hammer the shape flat. Use round-nose pliers to make loops flush to the bottom front of the shape as shown.

Wrap 25" (63.5cm) of 34-gauge non-tarnish brass wire ten times around the top left of the pointed shape from Step 1, tucking the wire tail to the back of the shape. String on a red garnet bead and station it on the outer edge of the shape. Wrap the wire five times and string on another red garnet bead. Continue this pattern until you've used fifteen red garnet beads. Wrap the wire around the shape ten more times, and then cut the excess wire and tuck in the wire tail.

Starting at the top right side of the pointed shape, wrap 7" (18cm) of 22-gauge non-tarnish brass wire three times. String on a green pillow bead and station it to the front of the shape. Wrap two times, string on another green pillow bead, wrap two times, and then string on a third green pillow bead. Wrap three more times. Cut the excess wire and tuck in the wire tail.

Open the loops on the smaller shape from Step 3 and slide them into the loops at the top of the pointed shape. Close the loops.

Create twenty-five jump rings with 18-gauge non-tarnish brass wire and a 16mm dowel on the jump ring maker tool (see *Creating Jump Rings* on page 15). Use memory wire cutters to cut the rings from the coil and cut off any pointed ends so they're all flush. Hammer the rings flat on one side, and texture nine of them.

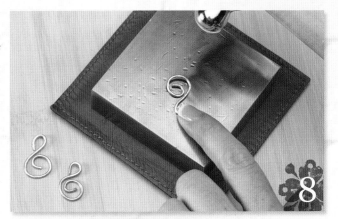

Using 2½" (6.5cm) segments of 18-gauge wire, create three ⅞" (2cm) spiral shapes with a loop at one end as shown. Hammer the shapes flat and add texture to one side. It's OK if the shapes are not all exactly the same shape and size.

Make an S-hook by bending a 4" (10cm) segment of 18-gauge non-tarnish brass wire around a ½" (1.5cm) mandrel (see *Creating a Hook and Eye Clasp* on page 16). Begin at the center of the wire and bend each end over the mandrel in the opposite direction, into an S-shape. Each bent segment should be approximately ¾" (2cm) long. Hammer the shape flat. Make a small loop in each end as shown.

Create eighteen coiled dangles from nine green pillow beads and nine black glass beads (see *Creating a Coiled Dangle* on page 20). Slide each bead onto a gold-plated head pin and make a coiled loop flush to the top of the bead.

Attach three pillow bead dangles to the loop on the focal shape using a manufactured 6mm jump ring (see *Opening and Closing Jump Rings* on page 15).

Create the necklace chain by attaching flat and hammered jump rings and spiral shapes in the following pattern: flat, hammered, flat, hammered, hammered, pair of flat links, hammered, pair of flat links, flat, hammered, flat, hammered, flat, hammered, flat, spiral shape, hammered, flat, hammered, flat, spiral shape, hammered, S-hook, flat, spiral shape, flat. Attach the final flat link to the left side of the top of the focal shape.

13 Attach three green pillow bead dangles to each of two 6mm jump rings. Attach these jump rings to the ninth link and the twenty-first link from the left side of the focal point. Attach three black glass bead dangles to each of three 6mm jump rings. Attach these jump rings to the sixth link, the eleventh link and the twenty-third link from the left side of the focal point.

VARIATION

These earrings started with an 18-gauge silver-plated wire formed into a smaller V-shape that was created with a pointed dowel and rounded edges. I took this shape and coiled it around the smaller area on my chasing hammer to create a three-dimensional spiral. I used a 24-gauge German-style silver-plated wire to wrap rose quartz tubes around the edge and 4mm coral rounds to the front, working around the periphery of the coiled earring shape.

By this chapter, you should be feeling really good about your progress. If you've stayed the course, you're well on your way to becoming a Wire Master. We're going to explore some more complicated ideas and build on your skills as we work towards the final chapter. I spent years coming up with innovative ways to use beading wire while working as a Beadalon Design Team member. I've taken the best of what I've discovered and added something new to the basic techniques to come up with pieces I hope will spark your creative imagination. Beading wire is surprisingly versatile, and with some trial and error, it's possible to use tension to force it into a variety of dimensional shapes. The key to all of these ideas is the tension created by having the right diameter of wire in the right sized bead hole, allowing you to build architecturally inspired pieces. Every time you change the beads, you'll need to experiment to find the right diameter of wire to make things work. That's the challenge, and I'm quite sure you're up to it!

Euclid (see page 86) is one of those ideas that happened completely by accident. As I was working with a simple double-needle ladder stitch, the wire began to curve naturally. I secured it with crimp beads, and a technique was born. Try this with other beads in different sizes and shapes and see what new creations you can concoct. *Amphritite* (see page 84) plays with ideas I've come to love in some new and different ways. Fringed wire, which usually dangles from necklaces, becomes a 3-D design element in the bracelet and adds kinetic movement. *Calder* (see page 100) is inspired by renowned artist Alexander Calder and plays with balance and kinetic movement. Using movement as a design feature makes for intriguing pieces that are delightful to wear.

Try each design, make changes in materials, scale and pattern, and use my ideas as springboards for your creativity. My entire goal in everything I do is to inspire you to take creative control and forge your own pathways. I'm just giving you a varied palette—you get to paint the masterpiece.

4 ARCHITECTURAL EXPLORATION
COMPLEX DIMENSIONAL BEADING WIRE AND BEAD DESIGNS

AMPHRITITE

This design features a fishnet pattern created with six different silver-plated beading wires. Sparkling crystals connect the wires, and fringe-like tendrils I call "fringles" add dimension and kinetic movement. Use different wire, smaller or larger beads, longer fringes or beaded fringes for a variety of finished effects.

Materials

49-strand .024" (0.6mm) silver-plated beading wire

eighteen size 2 silver-plated crimp tubes

eighteen SWAROVSKI ELEMENTS 4mm light sapphire rounds

four size 4 silver-plated crimp tubes

one silver-plated swivel lobster clasp

six SWAROVSKI ELEMENTS 8mm mocha rounds

ten SWAROVSKI ELEMENTS 8mm vintage rose rounds

twelve SWAROVSKI ELEMENTS 8mm fuchsia rounds

two 6mm silver-plated jump rings

Tools

flush cutters

Mighty Crimp Tool

two pairs of chain-nose pliers

Finished Length: 8" (20.5cm) to fit a 7" (18cm) wrist

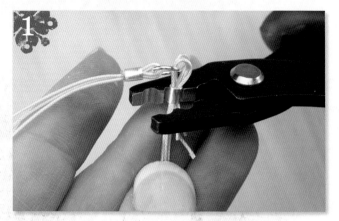

Thread three 9" (23cm) segments of silver-plated beading wire through a size 4 crimp tube and a 6mm jump ring, and then back into the crimp tube. Crimp and trim the excess wires (see *Using a Crimp Tool* on page 17). Repeat this step with another three 9" (23cm) segments, but thread them through the same 6mm jump ring.

String a fuchsia round onto the two outer strands of wire on each side of the bracelet. String a mocha round onto the two center strands.

Using the inner four strands, string a vintage rose round on the left two strands and the right two strands as shown.

Repeat Steps 2 and 3 until you reach the eleventh and twelfth fuchsia rounds. Thread a size 4 crimp tube onto three of the wires and through a 6mm jump ring, and then back through the crimp tube. Crimp. Repeat for the remaining three wires, threading them through the same 6mm jump ring. Attach a lobster clasp to the jump ring.

Cut nine 1" (2.5cm) beading wire segments. Thread a segment into the second mocha round. String a light sapphire round onto each wire end. Secure the segment and beads with a size 2 crimp tube on each side, crimping with chain-nose pliers. Repeat this step on the fourth and sixth fuchsia and mocha beaded sections.

EUCLID

I'm always attempting to create new sculptural concepts with beading wire, and this one happened while playing with double-needle ladder stitch. The diameter and strand count of the wire had the perfect tension to turn in on itself and form a triangular shape when threaded through the crystal bicones. I went with it and made small wire segments that I strung onto a core wire for a really interesting bracelet.

Materials

7-strand .018" (0.5mm) purple beading wire

four 6mm silver-plated jump rings

four silver-plated head pins

one silver-plated lobster clasp

ten SWAROVSKI ELEMENTS 6mm rose bicones

thirteen SWAROVSKI ELEMENTS 6mm indicolite bicones

thirteen SWAROVSKI ELEMENTS 6mm padparadscha AB bicones

thirteen SWAROVSKI ELEMENTS 6mm violet AB bicones

thirty size 2 silver-plated crimp beads

two silver-plated loop crimps

Tools

flush cutters

round-nose pliers

two pairs of chain-nose pliers

Finished Length: 7" (18cm)

Cut a 7" (18cm) segment of purple beading wire. String an indicolite bicone onto the center of the wire. String a second indicolite bicone onto one wire end; thread the other wire end through the same bicone in the opposite direction.

String a third indicolite bicone onto one wire end and thread the other wire end through the bicone in the opposite direction.

Thread both wire ends through the first bicone, going in opposite directions. Pull the wire tail and adjust the beads and wire to form a pyramid shape. Make all the loops in the pyramid shape equal in size.

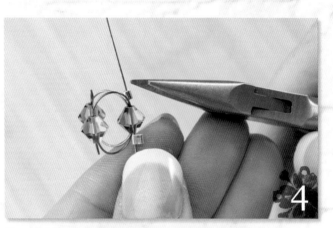

Thread a size 2 crimp bead onto each wire end. Crimp the beads flush against the first bicone using chain-nose pliers (see *Stationing Beads with a Crimp Tube* on page 19). Cut off the excess wires flush to the ends of the flattened crimp beads.

Repeat Steps 1–4 to create pyramid beads in the following colors: four violet, four padparadscha, four indicolite and three rose.

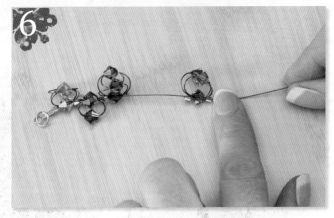

Thread an 8" (20.5cm) segment of beading wire into a loop crimp. Use chain-nose pliers to flatten the loop crimp end, securing the wire fully. String on the pyramid beads, separating each one with a crimp bead. Use the following color pattern: violet, padparadscha, indicolite, rose. Repeat this pattern until all pyramids have been used.

Thread the core wire into a second loop crimp end. Secure it with chain-nose pliers.

Attach a 6mm jump ring to one of the loop crimp ends (see *Opening and Closing Jump Rings* on page 14). Attach a second jump ring and a lobster clasp to the other loop crimp end.

Create a coiled dangle using each color of crystal bicone (see *Creating a Coiled Dangle* on page 20). String a crystal onto a head pin and make a coiled loop flush to the top of the bead. Trim the excess wire. Attach all four dangles to a single jump ring. Attach this jump ring to the jump ring containing the lobster clasp.

TIP I used purple wire, which gave me the correct tension for the pyramid beads. A wire in a different color might have the same gauge, but may produce an entirely different—and possibly undesirable—tension. The lesson? Experiment before using a different color wire in this project.

RADIUS

I started making little wire circles a few years ago, and I still find them endlessly fun. You can bead them, leave them naked or use a variety of colors and diameters of wire. No matter how you put it all together, there is a wonderful, open, airy quality to the design. You can take this wherever it leads you, and I suggest that you just enjoy the journey and not worry too much about the finish line.

Materials

18" (45.5cm) textured silver-plated chain

19-strand .018" (0.5mm) silver-plated beading wire

20-gauge silver-plated Artistic Wire

fifteen 3mm peridot rounds

five 1½" (4cm) silver-plated head pins

four ½" (1.5cm) silver-plated Quick Links rings

one 1" (2.5cm) silver-plated Quick Links ring

one small silver-plated toggle ring

one SWAROVSKI ELEMENTS 20mm crystal cosmic ring

seventeen 6mm silver-plated jump rings

twenty-six 4mm frosted peridot green cat's eye glass rondelles

twenty-two silver-plated size 1 crimp beads

two 5mm × 12mm yellow faceted teardrops

two 10mm carnelian flat discs

two 10mm olive jade flat discs

Tools

1" (2.5cm) mandrel

bench block pad

chasing hammer

flush cutters

round-nose pliers

steel bench block

two pairs of chain-nose pliers

Finished Length: 21½" (54.5cm)

Create six ¾" (2cm) diameter circles by forming a silver-plated beading wire segment into a circle shape and threading the ends into a size 1 crimp bead from opposite sides (see *Making Beading Wire Circles* on page 21). Compress the tube with chain-nose pliers and cut off the excess wire. Make two 1" (2.5cm) diameter circles and two ⅞" (2cm) diameter circles using the same process.

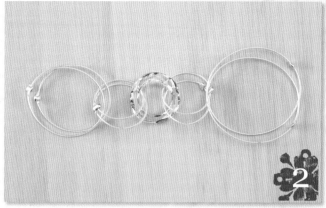

Form two ½" (1.5cm) diameter circles, but before crimping the circles closed, slide a crystal cosmic ring onto both circles. Form two more ½" (1.5cm) wire circles and thread them through the cosmic ring before crimping. Attach two ¾" (2cm) wire circles to the left side of this small chain, threading the segments through before crimping. Attach two 1" (2.5cm) wire circles to the right side of the chain, using the same technique. You should have a five-link chain segment made of wire circles and a crystal circle.

Create a beaded wire circle (see page 21) using fifteen cat's eye rondelles. Create a beaded wire circle using fifteen peridot rounds. Create a 1" (2.5cm) beaded wire circle with a cat's eye rondelle, a yellow faceted teardrop and ten more cat's eye rondelles.

Create coiled dangles using two with carnelian flat discs, two with olive jade flat discs and one with a yellow teardrop (see *Creating a Coiled Dangle* on page 20). Slide each bead onto a head pin and make a coiled loop flush to the top of the bead. Attach a 6mm jump ring to each coiled dangle (see *Opening and Closing Jump Rings* on page 14).

Begin constructing the necklace. You will be building the necklace from left to right. Connect the cat's eye rondelle beaded wire circle to the first link of the chain from Step 2 with a 6mm jump ring. Attach a ½" (1.5cm) Quick Link to the fourth link in the chain with a jump ring.

Connect a pair of ¾" (2cm) wire circles to the fifth link with a jump ring.

Connect the peridot beaded wire circle and the cat's eye/yellow teardrop beaded wire circle to another pair of ¾" (2cm) wire circles with a jump ring. Connect the circle pair to the necklace with a jump ring.

Attach an olive jade dangle to a pair of ¾" (2cm) wire circles with a jump ring. Attach this pair of wire circles to the necklace with another jump ring.

Attach a pair of ½" (1.5cm) circles and a yellow teardrop dangle to a pair of ⅞" (2cm) wire circles using a jump ring.

Connect two carnelian dangles and one jade dangle to a 1" (2.5cm) Quick Link with a single jump ring. Connect the Quick Link to the necklace with a jump ring.

Connect a pair of ½" (1.5cm) Quick Links to the necklace with a jump ring. One will flip over and dangle inside the previous link. Attach a ½" (1.5cm) Quick Link to one of the previous ½" (1.5cm) Quick Links in the necklace with a jump ring.

Attach a small toggle ring to the necklace with a jump ring.

Create a round hook clasp by shaping 20-gauge silver-plated wire around a 1" (2.5cm) mandrel. Use round-nose pliers to create loops in both ends. Hammer the clasp flat and texturize it with the ball peen end.

Match up two 9" (23cm) segments of silver-plated chain and connect each of the ends with a 6mm jump ring. Attach one end of the chain to the jump ring at the beginning of the necklace (containing the green cat's eye glass beaded wire circle). Attach the round hook clasp to the opposite side of the chain.

VARIATION

I used Crinkle Wire circles as connectors in this retro-fabulous bracelet. This is one of those "think of a different way to use a technique" ideas. The Crinkle Wire makes wonderful, whimsical wired circles, and these vintage reproduction beads work perfectly in the design.

ORBITAL

These painted glass beads made me think of planets and spaceships, and thus this orbital concept was born. I like the bold simplicity of red, black and white here, and the wires moving in and around the beads lend movement and dimension. I'm truly enamored of these beading wire dangles, and now that I've started making them I'm afraid I can't stop!

Materials

7-strand .018" (0.5mm) black beading wire

7-strand .018" (0.5mm) satin silver beading wire

eight 6mm black obsidian faceted rounds

eight 15mm painted Czech glass spaceship beads

five size 2 crimp tubes

four 6mm white agate faceted pillow beads

four 8mm black obsidian faceted rounds

four 9mm × 17mm white agate puffed rectangle beads

four 10mm black obsidian faceted rounds

one small silver-plated toggle clasp

three 6mm silver-plated jump rings

twenty-two 8mm white agate rounds

two size 3 crimp tubes

Tools

flush cutters

Mighty Crimp Tool

tape

two pairs of chain-nose pliers

Finished Length: 20" (51cm)

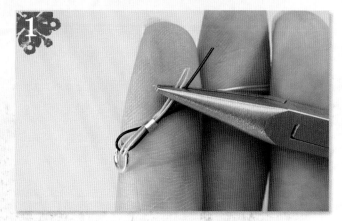

Thread two 24" (61cm) strands of satin silver beading wire and one 24" (61cm) strand of black beading wire through a size 3 crimp tube and a 6mm jump ring, and then back through the crimp tube. Chain-nose pliers are helpful when pulling the wires back through the tube. Crimp with the Mighty Crimp Tool (see *Using a Crimp Tool* on page 17) and cut off the excess wire tails flush to the bottom of the tube.

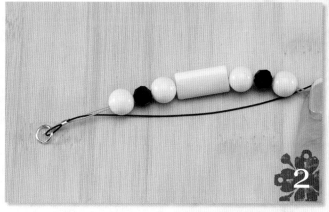

String a white agate round, a 6mm obsidian round, a white agate round, a white agate rectangle, a white agate round, a 6mm obsidian round and a white agate round onto the two silver strands.

String a spaceship bead onto both silver wires, an 8mm obsidian round onto one silver wire, a pillow bead onto both wires, a 10mm obsidian round onto one wire, a spaceship bead onto both wires, a 10mm obsidian round onto one wire, a pillow bead onto both wires, an 8mm obsidian round onto one wire, and a spaceship bead, a white agate round, a 6mm obsidian agate, a white agate round, an agate rectangle, a white agate round, a 6mm black agate and a white agate round onto both wires.

String a spaceship bead onto both silver wires. Repeat the pattern from Steps 2 and 3 for the other half of the necklace.

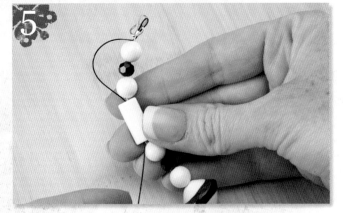

Tape the silver wire ends onto your workspace. Thread the black wire around the first three beads and into the first agate rectangle.

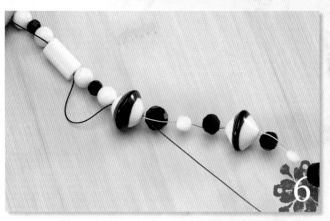

Thread the black wire around the next three beads and into the first spaceship bead.

Thread the black wire through every fourth bead in the strand. When you reach the final white agate round, remove the tape from the silver wires.

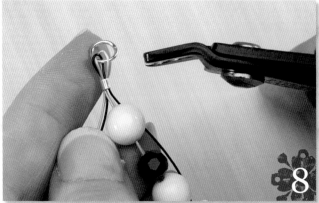

Thread all three wire ends into a size 3 crimp tube, through a 6mm jump ring, and then back into the tube. Crimp with the Mighty Crimp Tool. Cut the excess wire flush to the bottom of the tube.

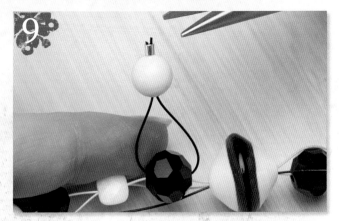

Cut a 2¼" (5.5cm) segment of black beading wire. Thread the wire through the first 8mm obsidian agate on the left side of the necklace. Thread both wire ends into a white agate round. Pull the wires through to create a 1" (2.5cm) long hot air balloon shape. Thread both wires through a size 2 crimp tube and crimp using chain-nose pliers. Cut off the excess wire tails. Repeat this process for the next 8mm obsidian round. On the opposite side of your necklace, thread the wires into the two 6mm obsidian rounds that line up with the 8mm obsidian rounds on the first half of the necklace.

Thread a 4¼" (11cm) segment of wire through the center spaceship bead. Thread both wire ends into a white agate round, a spaceship bead, a white agate round and a size 2 crimp tube. Form a 2" (5cm) long hot air balloon segment. Crimp both wire ends and cut off the excess wire.

Attach a toggle bar to one end of the necklace and a toggle ring attached to a jump ring to the other end of the necklace (see *Opening and Closing Jump Rings* on page 14).

GALAXY

Exposed sterling silver wire embellished with bronze freshwater pearls weaves in and out of a core strand of strawberry "quartz" glass and rust-colored, dyed quartz briolettes in this thoroughly modern design. The exposed wires can be evenly spaced or arranged in a random pattern as I've done here; it's entirely determined by your aesthetic. You can also opt to bead the exposed wire strands completely or omit the beads entirely.

Materials

49-strand .018" (0.5mm) .925 sterling silver beading wire

five 14mm × 20mm strawberry quartz glass oval beads

one large silver-plated lobster clasp

one small silver-plated toggle ring

seven size 3 silver-plated crimp tubes

twelve 5mm × 10mm dyed rust quartz briolette beads

twenty-six 6mm bronze free-form flat back freshwater pearls

two 6mm silver-plated jump rings

two silver-plated Scrimp findings

Tools

Scrimp tool

tape

two pairs of chain-nose pliers

wire cutters

Finished Length: 7¼" (18.5cm)

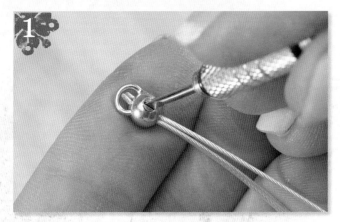

Attach a 7¾" (19.5cm) segment and two 14"(35.5cm) segments of sterling silver beading wire to a Scrimp finding using the Scrimp tool (see *Using a Scrimp* on page 18).

String a strawberry oval and three rust quartz briolettes onto the shorter wire. Continue stringing beads in this pattern until you reach the fifth strawberry oval. Tape the wire end to your work surface.

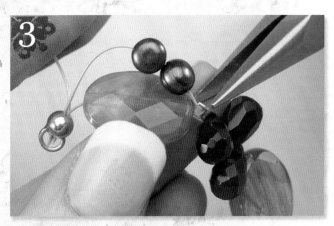

You will be alternating between the two 14" (35.5cm) wires that remain. Thread the first wire with two pearls and a size 3 crimp tube. Bring this wire over the first strawberry oval and thread it through the first briolette. Use chain-nose pliers to crimp the tube, securing the pearls.

String two pearls onto the second wire and thread it into the third briolette. Add a crimp tube. Before crimping the tube, pull the wire out a little so it has an arc.

String two pearls and a crimp tube onto the first wire. Thread the wire through the first briolette in the second section. Crimp the tube with chain-nose pliers, securing the pearls.

String three pearls onto the second wire and thread it through the first briolette in the third section. Before crimping the tube, pull the wire out a little so it has an arc.

String six pearls onto the first wire through six pearls and a crimp tube. Thread it through the first briolette in the final section. Crimp. String five pearls onto the second wire and then thread it through the third briolette on the last segment. String on a crimp tube and crimp.

Thread the two open wires with three pearls each. Untape the remaining wire and thread all three wires through a Scrimp finding. Close the Scrimp with the Scrimp tool. Cut off the excess wires.

Attach a 6mm jump ring and a lobster clasp to one end of the bracelet and a jump ring and a toggle ring to the other end of the bracelet (see *Opening and Closing Jump Rings* on page 14).

CALDER

There are certain fine artists who I find endlessly inspirational, and Alexander Calder is one of them. I don't think most people realize that beyond the kinetic mobiles he is most known for, Calder also created jewelry. His approach to working with wire inspired the essence of this book, dimensional and sculptural designs constructed from wire forms. I find him fascinating. I wanted to capture the spirit of a Calder mobile in a beading wire design. You can thread the focal wires in a variety of manners to different effect, so play with this idea!

Materials

49-strand .024" (0.6mm) .925 sterling silver beading wire

fifteen size 3 silver-plated crimp tubes

four 10mm silver-plated jump rings

four silver-plated pinch bails

nine 6mm × 7mm dyed hot pink jade barrel beads

one silver-plated toggle clasp

sixteen 6mm × 9mm dyed aqua jade briolettes

thirteen 7mm × 10mm dyed hot pink jade briolettes

three 6mm silver-plated jump rings

two Scrimp findings

Tools

flush cutters

Scrimp tool

two pairs of chain-nose pliers

Finished Length: 17" (43cm)

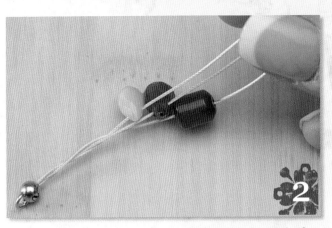

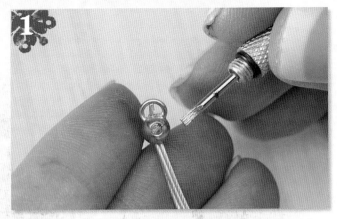

Cut three 28" (71cm) segments of sterling silver beading wire. Attach all three to a Scrimp finding using the Scrimp tool (see *Using a Scrimp* on page 18). Cut off the excess wire.

Braid the wires six times; string an aqua briolette onto the first wire, a hot pink briolette onto the second wire and a hot pink barrel onto the third wire.

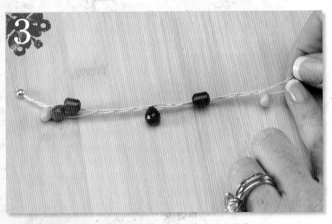

Braid the wires six times. String a hot pink briolette onto one wire. Braid six times, and then string a hot pink barrel onto one wire. Braid six times, and then string an aqua briolette onto one wire. Work the full pattern from Steps 2 and 3 two more times, but on the last repeat, omit the aqua briolette. End by braiding the wires six times.

Attach all three wires to a Scrimp finding using the Scrimp tool. Cut off the excess wire with flush cutters.

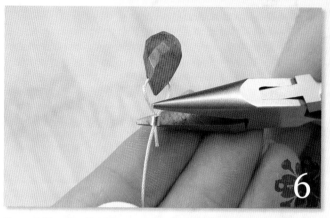

String a size 3 crimp tube and a hot pink briolette on a 2¼" (5.5cm) segment of wire. Thread the wire back into the tube and crimp with chain-nose pliers. Cut off the excess wire tail flush to the bottom of the crimp.

Repeat Step 5, attaching a second pink briolette to the opposite end of the wire segment.

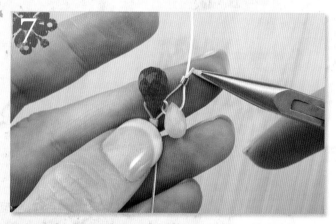

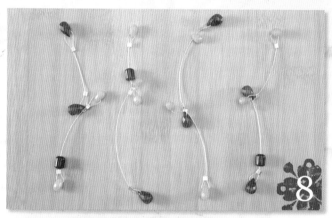

String a crimp tube and an aqua briolette onto a 3" (7.5cm) segment of wire and crimp as before. Thread the wire into one of the loops on the hot pink briolette wire segment from Steps 5 and 6. String on a hot pink barrel bead. String on a crimp tube and an aqua briolette and crimp as before.

There are four beaded and crimped sections. The second is a 2¼" (5.5cm) segment with an aqua briolette on each end and a barrel bead in the center, threaded with a 3¼" (8.5cm) segment with an aqua briolette on one end and a pink briolette on the other. The third is a 3¼" (8.5cm) segment with hot pink briolettes on both ends and an aqua briolette in the center, threaded with a 2¼" (5.5cm) segment with an aqua briolette on each end. The fourth is a 2½" (6.5cm) segment with an aqua briolette on each end, threaded with a 2¾" (7cm) segment with hot pink briolettes on each end and a barrel bead in the center. Follow the process from Steps 5–7 to assemble these sections.

Attach a pinch bail to the top of each wire segment. Attach each pinch bail with a 10mm jump ring to one of the wires in the braided core necklace, near the four center beads, as shown (see *Opening and Closing Jump Rings* on page 14).

Attach a 6mm jump ring and a toggle ring to one side of the necklace and two 6mm jump rings and a toggle bar to the other side.

VARIATION

These earrings employ a similar concept as the necklace. I threaded two beading wires into a crimp tube and added a different size and weight briolette on each wire. One is a fiery red CZ and the other is a yellow quartz, both gifts from a good friend. The dark blue dyed rondelles give another dimension to the design. These are really stunning on the ear.

Well, you're almost there, my friend. Give yourself a pat on the back; you've earned it. We're taking everything we've learned so far and combining shaping and beading wire into sculptural masterpieces. Nothing here is too tough, I promise; it's all just a matter of doing things a little differently and putting it all together. Combining beading and shaping wire opens up a new realm of possibilities. They can take turns in the center stage or combine their talents as a dynamic duo. No matter how you put it together, somehow it always works.

I absolutely love the vibrant colors in *Flamenco* (see page 106). This design is inspired by the ruffled skirts of flamenco dancers. Adding a woven hot pink crocheted wire accent really brings it all to life. *Chaos* (see page 109) was a result of an unplanned wire exploration. I was winding copper wire around my fingers and, suddenly, I found myself with an intriguing, open, free-form bead. A coordinated satin copper beading wire peeking through makes this necklace feel simultaneously modern and feminine. *Galahad* (see page 119) gives you just a taste of chain maille using jet black wires. You can take this technique as far as your patience will allow. There are ancient patterns of woven rings that will test your concentration skills greatly if you give them a try. Adding exposed wire links provides a modern take on an old idea.

Once you finish this chapter, I'm hopeful that you'll have a newly acquired passion for working with wire. You will have graduated—congratulations! I think sometimes it's easy to relegate wire to a supporting role, but there is so much you can do with it if you cast it as the star. I am endlessly inspired and excited by the challenges that working with wire present to me. It's just a wee little bit of an obsession, forcing a hopelessly impatient girl to focus and slow down. Hopefully, it will become an obsession for you, too.

5

THE FIFTH DIMENSION

COMBINING BEADING AND SHAPING WIRE DESIGNS

Hot pink and vivid orange beads dance around your wrist in this mixed-media bracelet design. The color palette and scale can be changed to suit your tastes. Crocheted shaping wire gives the core bracelet structure, while the dangling filigree flowers give the design a decidedly whimsical appeal.

Materials

22-gauge rose Artistic Wire

22-gauge tangerine Artistic Wire

49-strand .018" (0.5mm) beading wire

five 14mm bright orange plastic rounds

five 14mm magenta plastic rounds

one 1¼" (3cm) bright tangerine plastic reproduction vintage German filigree

one 5mm soft pink cat's eye glass rondelle

one large silver-plated toggle clasp

three 1¼" (3cm) hot pink plastic reproduction vintage German filigrees

three 5mm deep orange cat's eye glass rondelles

three 6mm silver-plated jump rings

two silver-plated EZ-Crimp ends

Tools

5.5mm crochet hook

chain-nose pliers

flush cutters

Mighty Crimp Tool

round-nose pliers

Finished Length: 7¾" (19.5cm) to fit a 7" (18cm) wrist

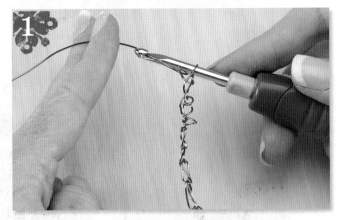

Work from the spool. Crochet a 12" (30.5cm) segment of chain stitches using 22-gauge rose wire. Don't remove the chain from the spool until you are sure it will fit the entirety of your bracelet. You may need to crochet more wire so it will fit your beads.

Create a small loop in a 1" (2.5cm) segment of 22-gauge tangerine wire and thread it through an orange rondelle and the center of a hot pink filigree. Use round-nose pliers to form a larger loop flush to the bottom of the filigree. Make three hot pink filigree components. Make one tangerine filigree component using rose wire and a pink rondelle.

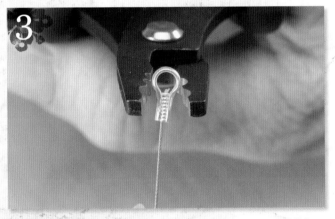

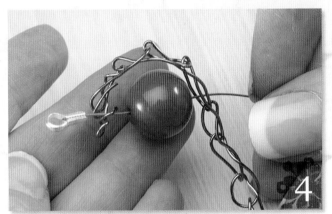

Attach a 10" (20.5cm) segment of beading wire to an EZ-Crimp end using the Mighty Crimp Tool (see *Using an EZ-Crimp* on page 18).

Slide the first chain stitch of the crocheted wire and a magenta round onto the beading wire. Gently frame the top of the round with the crocheted wire. Thread the beading wire through the crochet stitch that is flush to the bead hole on the other side. Always choose the smallest opening in the crocheted wire. This is so the crocheted wire will fit snugly around the beads.

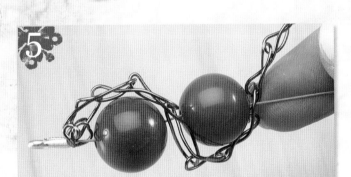

Thread on a bright orange round. Frame the bottom of the bead with the crocheted wire and thread the beading wire into the stitch that is flush to the bead hole on the other side.

Continue this S-pattern, alternating bead colors until you reach the tenth bead. Frame the crocheted wire around the tenth round and thread the core wire through the stitch that is flush with the bead hole. Use wire cutters to cut the excess crocheted wire, leaving a small wire tail. Tuck the wire tail into the chain using chain-nose pliers. Thread the core wire into an EZ-Crimp. Use the chain-nose pliers to tug the wire through the crimp. Round the design before finishing to prevent it from being too stiff. Crimp with the Mighty Crimp Tool. Cut the excess core wire with flush cutters.

Attach a 6mm jump ring and a toggle ring to one end of the bracelet (see *Opening and Closing Jump Rings* on page 14). Attach two 6mm jump rings and a toggle bar to the other end.

Attach the loops on the back of the pink filigree components to the top stitch after the second pink round, the third pink round and the fourth pink round as shown.

Attach the loop on the back of the orange filigree component to the jump ring containing the toggle ring.

CHAOS

This free-form and organic design feels almost like a wire doodle, similar to the *Gerbera* project in that aspect and yet, as you can see, entirely different in the execution. I love the open feeling this evokes and the way the satin copper wire is suspended in the wire cages. Chartreuse is a lovely color to pair with copper. I'm completely smitten with this design.

Materials

18-gauge copper Artistic Wire

19-strand .018" (0.5mm) satin copper wire

20-gauge copper Artistic Wire

ten 8mm acid green dyed jade nuggets

two 6mm copper jump rings

two copper bead covers

two size 2 crimp tubes

Tools

bench block pad

chasing hammer

Mighty Crimp Tool

round-nose pliers

steel bench block

standard crimp tool

two pairs of chain-nose pliers

Finished Length: 18" (45.5cm)

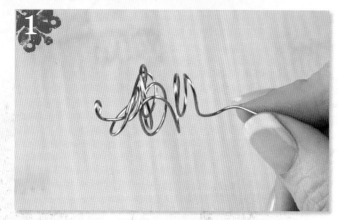

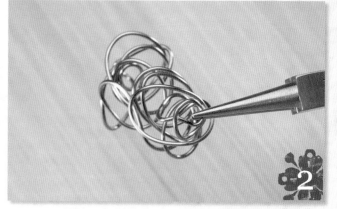

Work from the spool. Make a small loop at the end of the 20-gauge copper wire using round-nose pliers. Begin coiling the wire in a free-form manner. Loop the wire around and around, make funky loops and change directions. Don't overthink this!

When the loop segment is about 1¼" (3cm) long, cut the wire and use round-nose pliers to make a small loop in the opposite end. The loops will help secure the segments on the core beading wire.

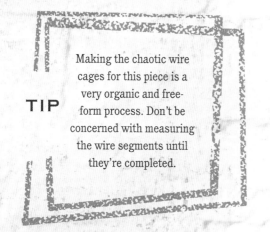

TIP

Making the chaotic wire cages for this piece is a very organic and free-form process. Don't be concerned with measuring the wire segments until they're completed.

Adjust the loops on either end of the wire with chain-nose pliers, making them flush to both ends of the shape; this forms a tube. Repeat Steps 1–3 to create nine wire cages.

Thread a 20" (51cm) piece of copper beading wire through a size 2 crimp tube and a 6mm jump ring, and then back through the crimp tube. Conceal the tube with a copper crimp cover. Use the jaws of a Mighty Crimp Tool to gently secure the cover around the crimp tube (see *Using a Crimp Tool* on page 17).

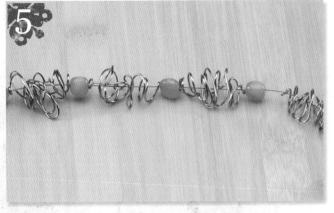

Alternate stringing jade beads and wire cages, ending with the tenth jade bead.

Thread the wire end through a crimp tube and a jump ring, and then back through the crimp tube. Cover the tube with a crimp cover and crimp.

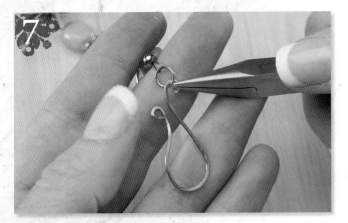

Make a 1¼" (3cm) long hook clasp from 18-gauge copper wire (see *Creating a Hook and Eye Clasp* on page 16). Hammer the clasp using a chasing hammer and a steel bench block. I really hammered this one flat so it was super sturdy and work-hardened. Use the ball peen end of the chasing hammer to apply texture. Attach the hook to one of the jump rings on the necklace. This design looks fabulous when worn asymmetrically.

VARIATION

This bracelet features the same technique applied to cool colored wires. The use of multiple colors adds a funky appeal. I used a purple beading wire for the core wire and coordinated SWAROVSKI ELEMENTS crystals to pull it all together. The wire beads can be made shorter or longer, and if you use a dowel you can even alter the shape.

MESOPOTAMIA

Gunmetal wire in a 16-gauge is shaped and hammered flat. A glass bead is wired in between the spaces, and black beading wire stands in for horse hair in this Iron Age-inspired design. I was visualizing hand-forged jewelry made with primitive materials to be worn by a warrior priestess.

Materials

16-gauge gunmetal Artistic Wire

26-gauge gunmetal Artistic Wire

49-strand .018" (0.5mm) black beading wire

twenty-eight size 2 gunmetal crimp beads

two 3mm baby blue Czech glass teardrops

Tools

bench block pad

chain-nose pliers

chasing hammer

flush cutters

round-nose pliers

steel bench block

WigJig tool

wire rounder tool

Finished Length: 4" (10cm) from top of ear wire to bottom of fringe

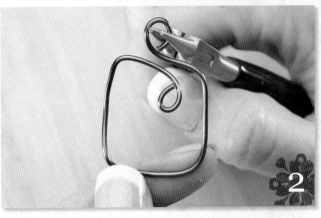

Arrange six pegs in the WigJig tool as shown (see *Using a Wire Jig* on page 19). Cut a 5" (12.5cm) piece of 16-gauge gunmetal wire. Wrap one end of the wire around the top peg. Wrap the wire around the outer pegs, compressing it to form the square shape. Wrap the wire tail around the center peg as shown. Remove the shape from the jig and cut off the excess wire.

Use round-nose pliers to shape the loops at the top and inside of the square. Use a chasing hammer and a steel bench block to flatten the wire shape.

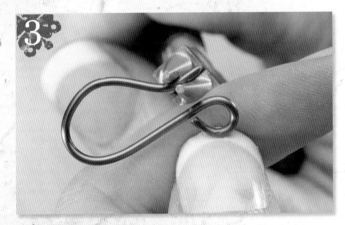

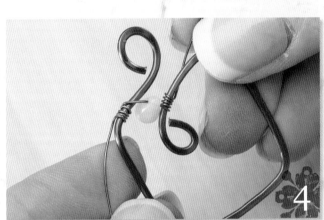

Use a 2" (5cm) piece of 16-gauge gunmetal wire to create a French-style ear wire (see *Creating an Ear Wire* on page 16). Loop one end of the wire, bend the wire at the midway point over your index finger, and then bend the end up slightly. Cut off the excess wire. Use a wire rounder tool to smooth the end. Use the chasing hammer and steel bench block to hammer the loop and the bend in the ear wire flat.

Begin wrapping an 8" (20.5cm) section of 26-gauge gunmetal wire just above the top bend on the left side of the square shape as shown. Wrap four times. String a baby blue teardrop onto the wire so it bridges the gap in the shape. Wrap the 26-gauge wire around the opposite wire in the square four times as shown. Cut off the excess wire. Tuck the wire tails under using chain-nose pliers.

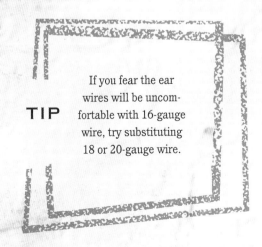

TIP If you fear the ear wires will be uncomfortable with 16-gauge wire, try substituting 18 or 20-gauge wire.

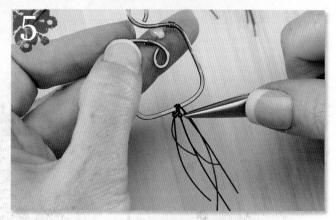

Cut a 3½" (9cm) section of black beading wire. Fold the wire over the bottom opening in the square shape. Thread both wire ends into a size 2 crimp bead and use chain-nose pliers to secure the crimp bead closed, close to the square shape but not so flush that the wire can't dangle. Repeat for fourteen "fringles" on the square shape. The wire ends should be slightly different in length, but not dramatically different.

Attach an ear wire to the square using chain-nose pliers. Repeat Steps 1–6 for the second earring.

VARIATION

This African-inspired bead and wire choker uses white beading wire, rubber tubing, head pins and a memory wire base. These fringle elements work in so many unexpected ways, and you can create loops or fringes and add beads for texture. This necklace never fails to garner compliments.

CARNAVALE

Creating this whimsical design was a very organic process. I have a large number of old keys and a huge collection of vintage buttons. The juxtaposition of the bright buttons with the distressed keys and gunmetal wire creates a retro feeling. Like something that is old and yet new, yes? Hunt down some unique buttons and combine them with the keys and beads in any way you choose. Use the steps as a guide as you create your own unique design.

Materials

.018" (0.5mm) satin copper beading wire

20-gauge gunmetal Artistic Wire

22-gauge gunmetal Artistic Wire

approximately thirty ½" (1.5cm) plastic buttons with two to four holes in various colors

four ⅞" (2cm) plastic buttons with two to four holes in various colors

four 6mm–8mm rounds

one silver-plated spring ring clasp

six 10mm silver-plated jump rings

three vintage metal keys

twelve 3mm–4mm rounds

twenty-five 8mm white agate rounds

two 6mm silver-plated jump rings

two silver-plated loop crimp ends

Tools

electric drill with ¹⁄₁₆" (2mm) bit

permanent marker

round-nose pliers

two-hole punch

two pairs of chain-nose pliers

wire cutters

Finished Length: 18" (45.5cm)

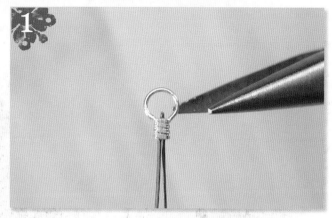

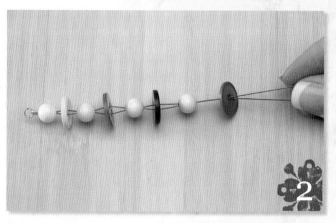

Cut two 24" (61cm) strands of satin copper beading wire. Thread them into a loop crimp and crimp with chain-nose pliers.

String a white agate bead onto both wires. Thread each wire through a hole in a ½" (1.5cm) button with two to four holes. Thread both wires into a white agate bead. Alternate between buttons and beads in this manner until you have used twenty-four buttons. End with an agate bead through both wires. Thread the wire ends through a loop crimp end and crimp with chain-nose pliers. Trim the excess wire.

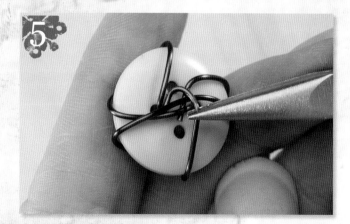

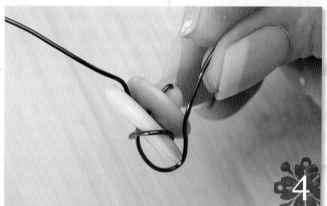

Cut an 8" (20.5cm) piece of 20-gauge gunmetal wire. String a 6mm–8mm round onto the center of the wire and bend both wire ends down. Thread each wire end through a hole in a ½" (1.5cm) button, and then through the holes in a ⅞" (2cm) button.

Free-form wrap the wire ends into and around the button layers to secure them.

Secure the wire ends at the back of the button component by tucking them in with chain-nose pliers. Repeat Steps 3–5 to make four button components.

Using an electric drill and a 1/16" (2mm) bit, drill a hole in the top of each button component.

Using a permanent marker, mark four dots equidistant along the top edges of a metal key. Drill four holes with a two-hole punch.

TIP I used hexagonal keys, which made marking easier, but you can use any key you'd like. Even better, use skeleton keys and skip the drill altogether.

Cut an 8" (20.5cm) piece of 22-gauge gunmetal wire. Place a 1/2" (1.5cm) button on top of the key and begin securing it with the wire, using the four drilled holes to weave from front to back and back to front. Twist and secure the wire ends with chain-nose pliers in the back.

Wrap another 8" (20.5cm) piece of 22-gauge gunmetal wire tightly around the top of the base of the key. Cut off the excess wire and tuck in the tail.

Working from the top of the base of the key, begin wrapping 22-gauge gunmetal wire around the key base, stringing on up to four 3mm–4mm beads. Secure the wire at the bottom, cut off the excess and tuck in the wire tail. Repeat Steps 8–10 to make two more key components.

Attach the button components to the necklace by threading a 10mm jump ring through the previously drilled hole in the top (see *Opening and Closing Jump Rings* on page 14). Attach the key embellishments in the same way, using the natural hole in the key. Start in the center of the necklace and attach a key component. Use the picture as a guide for placement of the remaining components.

Attach a 6mm jump ring to the loop crimp ends at each end of the necklace. Attach half of a spring ring clasp to each jump ring.

VARIATION

I used some lovely La Mode from Blumenthal Lansing coordinate buttons stacked and wire wrapped to create these earrings. I carried the colors to the crystal accents, and the modern pinch bail and earring components continue the circular theme of the buttons. This design has a completely different feel from the rustic appeal of the necklace.

GALAHAD

A chain maille section is connected to beading wire figure-eight links in this kinetic and kicky little bracelet. Consider making an entire bracelet of either section. Chain maille has been around for centuries, and making it involves a meditative process of weaving small jump rings into links. My patience level isn't high enough to make an entire breastplate or headdress, but a bracelet section I can handle!

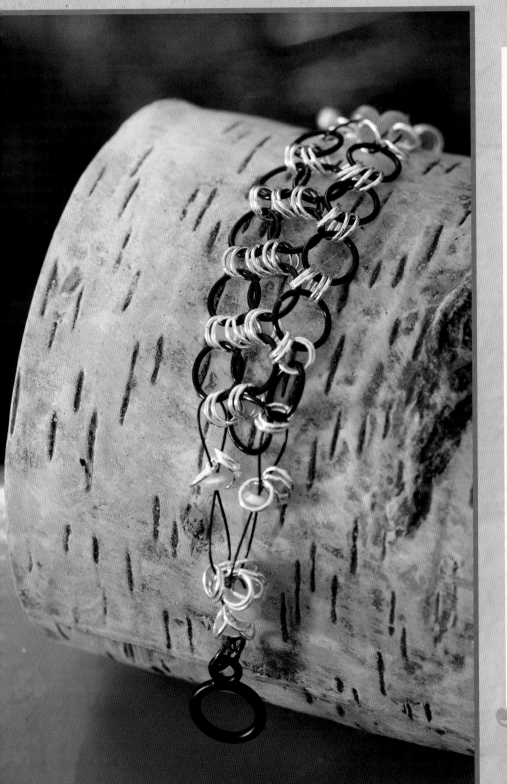

Materials

7-strand .018" (0.5mm) black beading wire

18-gauge black Artistic Wire

eighty-four 5mm silver-plated jump rings

one 5mm gunmetal jump ring

one 10mm gunmetal jump ring

one black toggle clasp

six size 2 black crimp beads

ten 6mm blue cat's eye glass rondelles

Tools

flush cutters

jump ring maker tool with 8mm dowel

two pairs of chain-nose pliers

Finished Length: 7" (18cm)

Create black jump rings on a jump ring maker tool using 18-gauge Artistic Wire (see *Creating Jump Rings* on page 15). Cut the coil from the tool. Cut fifteen jump rings from the coil. Use flush cutters to cut both ends flush.

Make a single chain of five black jump rings, each connected by two 5mm silver-plated jump rings (see *Opening and Closing Jump Rings* on page 14). Repeat this step to make two more chains.

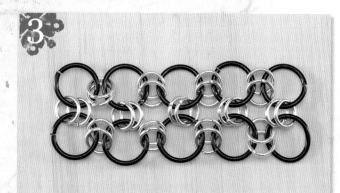

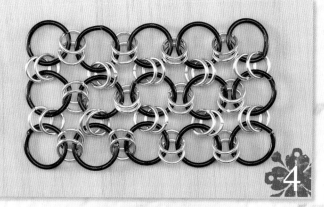

Attach the first two chains together using two jump rings to connect each corresponding ring on each chain length.

Repeat Step 3 to attach the third chain in the same fashion.

TIP If you get lost in the pattern, place the fabric flat so you can find your way back!

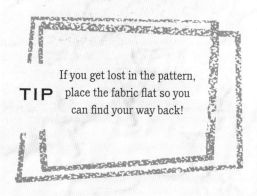

Cut a 5" (12.5cm) segment of black beading wire. Thread four 5mm silver-plated jump rings onto the wire. Thread the wire into the top jump ring on one side of the chain maille section. Thread both strands into a blue cat's eye rondelle.

Thread two 5mm silver-plated jump rings on each wire. Thread the wires from opposite ends into a size 2 crimp bead. Crimp with chain-nose pliers. Cut off the excess wire.

Repeat Steps 5 and 6 to make another figure eight in the other corner ring.

Thread a 2½" (6.5cm) segment of beading wire through the top of both figure eights. String a blue cat's eye rondelle and two jump rings onto each wire end. Thread both wire ends through a blue cat's eye rondelle. Thread a 5mm gunmetal jump ring onto one wire end. Thread both wires into a crimp bead and crimp. Cut off the excess wire.

Repeat Steps 5–8 for the opposite side of the bracelet; however, in Step 8, use a 10mm gunmetal jump ring instead of a 5mm jump ring.

Attach a toggle bar to the 5mm gunmetal jump ring at one end of the bracelet. Attach the toggle ring to the other end. Check all jump rings to ensure that they are securely closed.

TRIAD

This design has been rolling around in my noggin for several years. I wanted to find a way to create the right tension so that three beads would form a pyramid shape, which proved easier said than done. Previous attempts almost worked, but the beads slipped out of formation when the piece was handled. It occurred to me that free-form wrapping wire around each tube would shorten the three wires enough to maintain the pyramid shape. I added a chain and clasp to give you two options: necklace or bracelet. You can create this piece with round or square beads; truth be told, round beads are more comfortable if you opt to wear it as a bracelet.

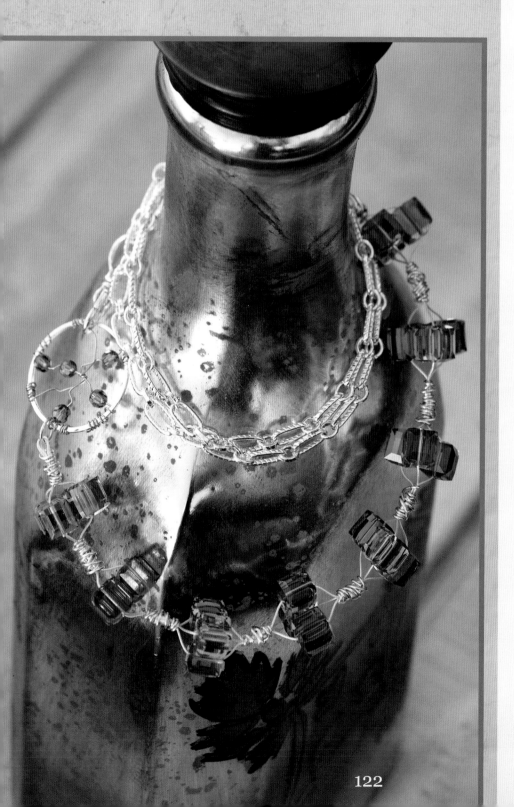

Materials

.020" (0.5mm) silver-plated beading wire

19" (48.5cm) textured long and short silver-plated chain

22-gauge silver-plated German-style wire

24-gauge silver-plated Artistic Wire

five SWAROVSKI ELEMENTS 4mm light topaz faceted rounds

one 1" (2.5cm) silver-plated Quick Links ring

one 10mm silver-plated jump ring

one silver-plated swivel lobster clasp

seven size 4 silver-plated crimp tubes

three 6mm silver-plated jump rings

twelve SWAROVSKI ELEMENTS 8mm light topaz cubes

twelve SWAROVSKI ELEMENTS 8mm violet cubes

two silver-plated Scrimp findings

Tools

flush cutters

Mighty Crimp Tool

round-nose pliers

two pairs of chain-nose pliers

Finished Length: 19½" (49.5cm) as a necklace; 8½" (21.5cm) as a bracelet, to fit a 7" (18cm) wrist

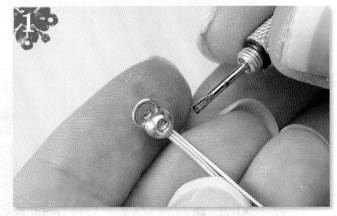

Attach three 14" (35.5cm) segments of silver-plated beading wire to a Scrimp finding using a Scrimp tool (see *Using a Scrimp* on page 18).

Thread a violet cube onto each wire. Thread all three wires into a size 4 crimp tube. Station the beads in a pyramid formation, and then crimp the tube with the Mighty Crimp Tool (see *Using a Crimp Tool* on page 17).

Repeat Step 2, alternating sets of three light topaz cubes with sets of three violet cubes, stationing a crimp tube in between each. When you reach the eighth set, thread all three wires into a Scrimp finding and secure with the Scrimp tool. Cut the excess wire with flush cutters.

Free-form wrap 8" (20.5cm) segments of 22-gauge German-style wire around the crimp tubes between the bead segments. Start in the center and wrap the wire to the left and right, creating tension on the three beading wires. Attach a 6mm jump ring to the Scrimp finding on each end of the beaded section (see *Opening and Closing Jump Rings* on page 14).

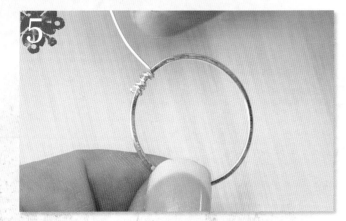

To create the dream catcher segment, wrap a 10" (25.5cm) segment of 24-gauge silver-plated wire around the edge of a 1" (2.5cm) Quick Link five or six times, leaving a small space between each wrap. Tuck the wire tail flush to the back of the circle with chain-nose pliers.

String on two light topaz rounds. Bring the wire across the interior of the Quick Link and wrap it around the opposite edge five or six times as before.

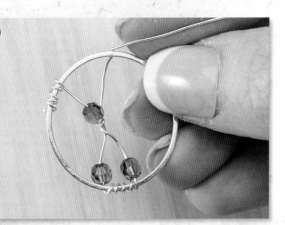

String a light topaz round onto the wire. Wrap it one time around the center of the wire that crosses the Quick Link, in between the first two beads, as shown. Bring the wire to an unwrapped edge of the Quick Link and wrap five or six times. Bring the wire to the center of the Quick Link and wrap it around the crossed wires once. Bring it to an unwrapped edge of the Quick Link and wrap five or six times.

String two more beads and bring the wire to the center. Wrap the wire around the crossed wires. Bring the wire to the opposite side and wrap five or six times. Cut the excess and tuck in the wire tail. Use round-nose pliers to secure the wires and beads by gently turning the wires and tightening the slack.

Attach the dream catcher to the jump ring at one end of the beaded section.

Attach a lobster clasp to the jump ring at the opposite end of the beaded section. When worn as a bracelet, let the dream catcher dangle.

Double over a 19" (48.5cm) segment of textured silver-plated chain. Attach a 10mm jump ring to the center of the chain. Thread a 10mm jump ring through both ends of the chain on the opposite side. Attach a lobster claw to the jump ring on one side of the chain. Attach this lobster claw to the dream catcher to make the piece a necklace.

TIP If you are using larger beads, take into account the inner diameter of your bracelet. The finished length may need to be larger than the length you usually wear. Measure it against your wrist as you work.

RESOURCES

The wire used in this book (with the exception of the annealed iron) was provided by Beadalon. Beadalon is the only wire manufacturer that cables, spools and packages their own wire, cable and strand for bead-stringing and wire-wrapping in their factories in the United States. They are the undisputed industry innovator and strive continually to offer cutting-edge stringing and shaping wire as well as findings. As a former retail bead store owner and member of the Beadalon Design Team, I have been working with Beadalon wire for over twelve years. I prefer Beadalon stringing and shaping wire because it is high-quality, strong and supple, and comes in a wide variety of colors, finishes, gauges, diameters and strand counts. The beads used in the projects in this book came from a variety of sources. You can find both Beadalon wire and similar beads at your local craft and jewelry-making supply stores, as well as online.

INDEX

GOT WIRE ON THE BRAIN?
GET WRAPPED UP IN JEWELRY TITLES
FROM NORTH LIGHT BOOKS.

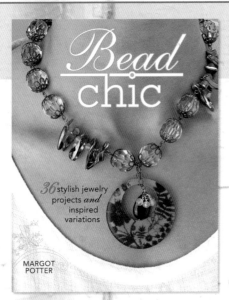

BEAD CHIC

36 STYLISH JEWELRY PROJECTS AND INSPIRED VARIATIONS
Margot Potter

Bead Chic will show you how to take inspiration that you love and forge your own creative path. After learning basic jewelry techniques, you'll be launched into 36 gorgeous projects. Each project comes with a variation, so you'll learn how easy it is to adapt virtually any project to suit your individual style, making you your own designer. You'll get to play with beads, a variety of stringing materials—from coated wire, to shapeable wire to commercial chain—and findings, all easily found at local and online craft retailers.

paperback; 8" × 10"; 128 pages
Z6942

MODERN EXPRESSIONS

CREATING FABULOUS AND FASHIONABLE JEWELRY WITH EASY-TO-FIND ELEMENTS
Fernando DaSilva

Inside *Modern Expressions* you will find chic necklace, earring and bracelet designs that turn heads with their fashion-forward sensibility. This book goes beyond instruction for creating striking pieces and helps you see clothing options to pair with the jewelry, with a how-to wear sidebar accompanying at least half of the projects. All of the projects feature modern components provided by major manufacturers (such as Beadalon), so locating supplies will be easy and painless.

paperback; 8.25" × 10.875"; 128 pages
Z7616

BEAD & WIRE JEWELRY EXPOSED

50 DESIGNER PROJECTS FEATURING BEADALON AND SWAROVSKI
Margot Potter, Fernando DaSilva and Katie Hacker

Bead & Wire Jewelry Exposed features over 50 high-fashion jewelry pieces made using techniques that reveal typically hidden components. Beading wire, cording, findings, tubing and chain take center stage in these clever and designs. While the pieces may look complex, the techniques are simple enough for beginners—yet the designs are sophisticated enough for veteran jewelry crafters.

paperback; 8.25" × 10.875"; 144 pages
Z2508

These and other fine North Light titles are available at your local craft retailer, bookstore or online supplier, or visit our website at www.mycraftivitystore.com.